The Q.U.E.E.N Xperience

GUIDE TO PLAYING
YOUR ROYAL POSITION

Queen Collection

PRESENTING AUTHOR: MINISTER NAKITA DAVIS

Copyright © 2019 Minister Nakita Davis.

All rights reserved. No part of this publication may be reproduced, distributed, or transmitted in any form or by any means, including photocopying, recording, or other electronic or mechanical methods, without the prior written permission of the publisher, except in the case of brief quotations embodied in critical reviews and certain other noncommercial uses permitted by copyright law. For permission requests, write to the publisher, addressed "Attention: Permissions Coordinator," at the address below.

www.jesuscoffeeandprayer@gmail.com – Presenting Author Minister Nakita Davis

www.jesuscoffeeandprayer@gmail.com – Jesus, Coffee, and Prayer Christian Publishing House

Scriptures marked NIV are taken from the NEW INTERNATIONAL VERSION (NIV): Scripture taken from THE HOLY BIBLE, NEW INTERNATIONAL VERSION ®. Copyright© 1973, 1978, 1984, 2011 by Biblica, Inc.™. Used by permission of Zondervan

Scriptures marked NKJV are taken from the NEW KING JAMES VERSION (NKJV): Scripture taken from the NEW KING JAMES VERSION®. Copyright© 1982 by Thomas Nelson, Inc. Used by permission. All rights reserved

ISBN: 978-0-9998188-6-2

Chief Editor: Angel K. Fairley

Cover/Layout/Design: Eswari Kamireddy

Foreword by: Kim Honeycutt

Endorsements: Evangelist Latoya Mcdonald & Pastor Tammy Caesar

In loving Memory of Queen Co-Author

* * * * * * * * * * * * * * * * * * * *

Aliyah Terry

Spread Your Wings – Your Legacy Lives On!

Queen, you are Playing Your Heavenly Position

* * * * * * * * * * * * * * * * * * * *

Queen Table of Contents

In loving Memory of Queen Co-Author	iii
Foreword	vii
Endorsements	viii
A Note from the Chief Editor	x
Preface	xi
Prayer	1
Queen Poem	3
I Am Called By: Aliyah Terry (Smith)	4
Strength to the powerless By: Dr. Radisha Brown	12
Purpose Produces Promise By: Ja'nae Sturgis	19
It Hurts like Hell By: Tamika Morrow	26
The Secret *Purpose is your Birthright* By: Deborah Tulay	33
Trusting His Voice By: Sherry Jones	39
Weight of Why I Worship By: Evangelist Evonn Firms	45
Brittney Spears and Rock Bottoms By: Dominique Burleson	51
Ripple Effect By: Ashley Moraru	56
The Reason to Get Ready By: Tee Pringle	60
God's Extravagance, Presence, and Favor By: Colleen Batchelder	69
Bloom where you're planted By: Robyn Mobley	76
Who God Calls You to Be By: Aya Mhlongo	82
Prosper in the Lord By: Jessica Merino	88

God's Plan By: Ylonda Powell — 95

Afterword — 104

Thank you! — 107

Foreword

"Aliyah Terry is an inspiration for all, not because of her untimely death but because of time spent living for Jesus. If you want to **read real talk, raw emotions, and receive clear direction on how to use every life experience as a stepping stool for a renewed view, then this book is for you.** The partnership between Minister Nakita Davis and Aliyah Terry is palpable. Their writings together help all of us know how to keep it together. Aliyah's beautiful DNA is all over these pages. She lives on in her words because she stood on His."

Kim Honeycutt, MSW, LCSW, CCFC, LCAS
Psychotherapist, Founder, Speaker, & Author
www.butyourmotherlovesyou.com
www.kimhoneycutt.com
www.icuTalks.org

* * * * * * * * * * * * * * * * * * *

Endorsements

"The Q.U.E.E.N Xperience Guide to Playing Your Royal Position is a must read! These power-packed stories, testimonials and declarations gave me the boost needed to Play My Royal Position. I can't compare it to anything I've read before. Each story had a great level of transparency and gave me a relatable experience that encouraged me to keep moving forward in my own life. Thank you for your boldness to share your stories Queens!"

~Evangelist Latoya McDonald
Owner of My Out Loud, LLC
Www.myoutloud.com
Email: myoutloudmissions@gmail.com
FB & IG: My Out Loud Missions
Cashapp: $Latoyaoutloud

* *

"This book is refreshing for the Spirit as well as the mind. All the ladies possess an ability to overcome any life challenge. So, will you. Pass it on."

~Pastor Tammy Caesar

Pastor, Prophetess, Inspirational gospel singer/composer, & Niece to the legendary Shirley Caesar

http://www.tammycaesarministries.org/Pastor-Tammy-Caesar-Bio.html

* * * * * * * * * * * * * * * * * * * *

A Note from the Chief Editor

Open your hearts and minds and prepare to bask in the love and inspiration shared with the power of Our Father Jesus Christ shining through! If it touches your soul in some small measure, then we have accomplished our missions to enrich every aspect of your life.

Surely My Cup Runneth Over,

Angel K Fairley, Chief Editor

Jesus, Coffee, and Prayer Christian Publishing House

Preface

A note From the Publisher

Min. Nakita Davis ~ CEO & Founder

Jesus, Coffee, and Prayer Christian Publishing House & The Q.U.E.E.N Xperience women empowerment platform

Queen, you were designed for more – to do more and to be more in the body of Christ! You **were not** designed to play a small position, but to rise from the ashes and Play Your Royal Position.

Journey with me and a bevy of Queens who are taking strides and gaining wins in their homes, businesses, ministries, and nonprofit endeavors. Each Queen Co-Author journeyed through various obstacles, feelings of rejection, and moments of pain to BECOME the Queen she is today!

Be inspired by life changing nuggets of wisdom, inspiration, and the unique beauty that only God can bring in this blended royal court. Hear the testimonies from women in their twenties, thirties, forties, and beyond; women who are married, divorced, and single. Women with educational backgrounds ranging from high school diplomas to Doctorate degrees; women with children and women with none. Meet Mrs./Ms. Independents from Charlotte, NC to Michigan, from the Peach state of Georgia' to the shorelines of Jersey ~ and as far as Johannesburg, Africa too. This is an international movement!

Business savvy and spiritually led *Women of Black, White, and Spanish* heritage share The Q.U.E.E.N Xperience with love and sincerity ~ with the earnest hopes of empowering you to walk in your fullest potential.

Know that the women represented in this book are all on their individual journey – just like you and me. This is not a comparison tool, but rather an honest assessment of your current journey and where God has ordained you to be.

To fully appreciate this anthology, you must first understand what a Q.U.E.E.N represents.

Q. Quit making excuses

U. Understand your assignment

E. Enlist your supporting cast

E. Establish your winning team

N. Now

Each pillar replicates the ordained rise of Queen Esther and God's unwavering favor over her life during a time of adversity.

Queen Esther was the little cousin to Mordecai. He watched over her in her youth. She was smart, witty, and beautiful; despite her initial fear, she gained courage to lead the Israelites in victory against their enemies. Nuggets of gold can be gleaned from the life of this beautiful heroine of the Old Testament. I highly encourage you to put down your phone and pick up your bible to read her full story. *Esther 4*

My prayer is that you tap into your inner Esther.

Queen, it's time to drop all excuses.

Toss all that hinders. Learn how to vet a squad of biblically sound women who pray for you more than they talk about you, and who are *positioned and poised to help you crush your goals for anything God places in your path!* It's time that women in the body of Christ extend hands to support each ~ with **grace and intention** to catapult one another to the next dimension of our faith walk, our family talk, and all our business endeavors.

The era for 'mean girls' is over – It's time for real women to acknowledge their struggles but recognize that Our God is GREATER!

So, dig deep Queen; pull out your pen and notepad, and get ready to take notes.

I Declare and Decree, in Jesus Name, that This is your YEAR to Sparkle, Shine, and Pop in the body of Christ. Your gift, your talent, your voice, and your treasure, is so much Greater - even Greater than you will ever know!

When you obediently walk in your calling, fully equipped and with authority of the Holy Spirit, the winds have no choice but to obey your command.

Someone needs you to be bold.

Someone needs your testimony.

Someone needs to hear your struggle and your testament of triumph.

Someone needs to hear your failure but how the Grace of God sustained you during your valley low.

The Glory belongs to God; but He has already given you the victory through Christ Jesus!

Now, it's time for you to Level up.

I AM A Living Witness.

The world needs you Queen – needs the very thing that you've been holding back for years. The world needs that very ***thing*** to break generational curses, to suffocate doubt, to annihilate complacency, and to crush the enemy schemes!

There is No more room to be stuck and stagnant.

Chickens can walk but only Eagles take *flight*.

Queen you are an eagle – get ready to spread your wings and soar.

I believe in you. I'm fighting for you, praying for you, and rooting for your success NOW – In the name of Jesus Christ!

Queens Remember

"For if you remain silent at this time, relief and deliverance for the Jews will arise from another place, but you and your father's family will perish. And who knows but that you have come to your royal position for such a time as this?"

Then Esther sent this reply to Mordecai: "GO…."
Esther 4:14-16

My question is simple…

Queen Will You Go?

Queen Will You Move?

Queen, will you stir the pot, disrupt the status quo, and obey the Kingdom Calling over your life?

Queen, It's Time to Play Your Royal Position!

~Minister Nakita Davis

* * * * * * * * * * * * * * * * *

Prayer

Heavenly Father,

*O*n this day and every day, we thank you. You are so worthy to be praised. We thank you for your grace and your mercy. You have been better to us than we have been to ourselves.

Glory to Your Name Alone!

I come to you now asking that every heart, every mind, and every vessel that picks up this book, receives exactly what they need to drop every excuse, every naysayer, every lie, and every trick of the enemy. Remove every mental and physical hindrance that may delay or stop them from being great in the body of Christ. I cast down every witch, warlock, demon, and spirit that is not like you Father God – in their lives, the women who are represented in this book, and the women (and men) that belong to YOU!

I Speak BOLDLY, with All Authority in the Name of Jesus Christ, that generational curses will be broken off, negative thinking will dissipate, sin will no longer entangle, and a spirit of procrastination will cease. Your Light, Love, and Blessings will shine on every person earnestly seeking your FACE – your kingdom and righteousness in spirit and in truth!

Give your people a sound mind and a spirit of Hope! Let them rise from the ashes and build their homes with the stones that people, places, and situations have thrown at them. May they rise to their royal position for your Glory while here on earth – as in Heaven. I love you Lord and speak all these things and more in the Mighty Name of Jesus Christ! AMEN, AMEN, and AMEN.

~Minister Nakita Davis

Publisher/Queen Co-Author

* * * * * * * * * * * * * * * * *

Queen Poem

QUEEN

Her CONFIDENCE is not her own
It belongs to God

She prays for wisdom & discernment daily
She Lacks NOTHING

She freely gives
As she is blessed beyond measure

She has a sound mind &
Her steps are ordered

Her beauty is much deeper
Than what the naked eye can see

When many back down
She Stands up

Where many fall
She rises

Reaches back &
Plays Her Royal Position

Queen, It's Time to Play Your Royal Position
Min. Nakita Davis

* * * * * * * * * * * * * * * * * *

I Am Called

By: Aliyah Terry (Smith)

"Do not be quickly provoked in your spirit, for anger resides in the lap of fools." Ecclesiastes 7:9 NIV

I am Aliyah Terry (Smith), CEO of Savvy Strands Virgin Hair Co.

Since established in 2016, Savvy Strands has been providing luxurious extensions built to last with the proper maintenance.

Although, I have been able to operate a successful business, the road to success, has not been easy. Savvy Strands Virgin Hair launched in the midst of complete chaos in my life. I was lost, confused, angry, and hurt – mentally, emotionally, and more. It had been a year since I left "Corporate America" and I was beginning to regret leaving and taking on entrepreneurship full-time. I was in a state of lack. I was barely surviving, barely making ends meet, and the load was heavy. I felt lonely, but somehow I knew that I was never alone.

At this point, my marriage was very toxic in any and every way imaginable. Everything in my life was going downhill. ***God didn't bless my marriage, I did.***

I made the decision that it was time for us to be married because we were together for seven years, with two children. I knew I wasn't supposed to get married. On my wedding day, my six-year-old son pulled me to the side and begged me not to get married. He said that he loved me as his mom and he loved his dad, but we shouldn't get married. *From the mouths of babes*.

I know it was God trying to tell me.

But you know sometimes, ladies, we as women *ignore the signs* that we ask God to give us.

I began to think that I was *cursed*. Unspeakably bad things began to happen to me daily; it never got better only worse. I began losing things. Savvy Strands was not being marketed properly and we were not reaching our target market.

I was beginning to lose my faith and trust in God.

I knew Jesus Christ. I was raised in the church. But I looked at my surroundings and blamed everything going wrong in my personal life as the reason why my business was not expanding. At this point, I knew I had to quit making excuses on why things weren't going right. I knew exactly why my business – life wasn't flourishing. I was comfortable. Comfortable in my day to day situation – comfortable even in my mess. I had to overcome this state that was allowing me to accept things less deserving of me. It was drowning me and preventing me from getting to my greatness – the greatness that Jesus promised me. We all are destined for greatness; it is up to us to bring it out.

The first step to dropping my excuses was recognizing that I needed help. I wanted out of my comfortable wicked state, but I struggled on the how.

> I prayed to Jesus for help, guidance, and direction.

But every time I prayed I heard him loud and clear ask me to *pray for someone else.* I could hear Him telling me to 'tell someone else something.' I often became upset. I felt like *here I am pouring out my heart to Jesus,* **crying, pleading** for help; and his resolution is to help someone else? What about me God? Are you hearing me? I KNOW you see what's going on down here. I KNOW you know that my situation hasn't gotten any better – so why are you sending me to other people? I just couldn't understand.

Honestly, I tried to ignore His prompting and tried to "fix" things on my own. However, things got far worse before they got better. I had no peace. I had anxiety and physically could not sleep. I would pray repeatedly. Same results. I noticed many ladies going through similar difficult situations.

> ## I was so scared, but I knew that I had to listen to Jesus.

You see I already understood the calling on my life – to help people. But I wasn't willing to accept it. Helping people always gave me a great joyous and peaceful feeling. I would often get teased about it being called "a wannabe Mother Theresa." I love helping others, no reward in return needed. ***I didn't understand specifically how to help or who to help until that moment.***

> ## I am called to help young women.

What I was going through at that time was not only for my testimony, but to help the next young woman through her test. By sharing my testimony, I can be an intricate part of helping my community heal. Helping women heal just a little piece of hurt that they have encountered. That healing will help someone become a better woman for herself, a better mother for her children, and a better path on her journey to find her assignment in life.

Rising Above

It was time for me to gain my strength back. Time to stop letting my obstacles, opposition, anger, and lack of self-love hinder me from my ***greatness***. Things started to become clearer. I had to build myself up before I even thought about helping other women, and

> ## I couldn't find myself until I found Jesus.

I had to fall in love with Jesus. For me to find my way, I had to call on Jesus. Loving Him taught me how to ***love myself***, the **first**

step towards my greatness. The scripture that resonates with me regarding how God was able to turn my life around is Jude 1:20 ASV "But ye, beloved, building up yourselves on your most holy faith, praying in the Holy Spirit." Simply put, building myself up again required that I trust in God and fall in love with Jesus.

My biggest supporting cast and crew member is Jesus himself. I remember a situation where I had to quickly move my children and myself. *I took the last $100 to my name, packed my kids and my bags, grabbed my Savvy Strands Hair inventory and purchased 3 one-way Chinese bus tickets to NYC.*

I spent $90 on bus tickets and we moved to NYC with $10 in my pocket.

I prayed to God the entire way. I had no idea what I was doing but I trusted him the entire time. **I had nowhere for us to live once we arrived, no way of knowing how we would get food**; but even in all that I felt supported enough so that my faith immediately activated. Even though the situation was so wrong, God let me feel His love, His mercy and His forgiveness.

God is Love

My mother, lives in NYC and had given me the resources and guidance that I needed for myself and my children.

Who knew that that little piece of information would not only save my life but transition it for the greater good.

I needed support, guidance, and professional help in the form of counseling and therapy.

I reached out to a program as soon as we got to my mother's house around 11:30 am. Well God heard my prayers. The normal twenty-four-hour process for assistance turned out to take less than two hours for us! My children and I were placed in our temporary shelter housing and were provided with a list of FREE resources to help along our journey. For safety and protection purposes, I am unable to name my supporting resources – just know that they helped me in every way.

My winning team during this change in my life consisted of my best friend/sister, who lives in NYC as well. She was one of my biggest supporters during this transition because she kept me grounded and encouraged. She made sure I didn't forget about my business even through the toughest times. She even came up with the names of the next big thing that Savvy Strands will be introducing to the world. Hopefully, we will have this done by the time you are reading this. There was another best friend/big sister who would come up with ideas to expand Savvy Strands. It is always important to have someone on your winning team who is ready to act. Lastly, my business partner was a part of my support group. Even though she didn't handle the hair, she still treated Savvy Strands Hair like it was her baby too. When I was "homeless" at the time and couldn't afford marketing, she would help by making business cards, flyers, and delivering the hair to customers in the Charlotte area. I am so thankful and grateful to have a business partner such as her. *It is important to select the right people for your winning team because you're not going to feel like you're always winning.* There will be times when you feel like you are losing. In those times, you need positive people to motivate you and **remind you of your potential**.

Q.U.E.E.N Tip

Falling off track is easy. It takes no effort to detour off course. Just remember that you don't have to stay off course. With the right positive people on your winning team to help you get back on track, you can recover and achieve your goals. The right people understand that when 'One Wins – We All Win'.

After being in NYC for almost a year, life was good, and I could finally find the peace that I was longing for. I was happy and peaceful, but it wasn't great. I was content. **Remember, God promised us greatness.**

It was ironic, that the very place (NYC) where most people would have gone broke or given up all together, I was able to find my *peace*. Once I had my peace, I remembered my strength for the next level. Now I was ready to continue my fight. I moved back to Charlotte to receive everything God promised me, once I sought His face. "But seek ye first his kingdom, and his righteousness, and all these things shall be added to you." Matthew 6:33 ASV

Savvy Strands is NOW getting name recognition and getting more inquiries in Charlotte, NC. Savvy Strands now has a storefront location and with the help of God, will continue to profit abundantly. We are now receiving more inquiries in NYC and will hopefully be launching a storefront there soon. Father God Bless us with another successful location. Thank you in advance, Jesus.

Amen

About the Author

Aliyah Terry (Smith) was the LOVING mother of 2 beautiful children, a serial-entrepreneur, daughter, sister, friend, and CEO & Founder of Savvy Strands.

Sadly, her beautiful life was tragically cut short by domestic violence on July 2nd, 2019.

Just one day after the announcement of this collaborative book.

Although we mourn her life lost, we take this moment to celebrate Who she was in Jesus Christ. Aliyah lived life to the fullest and followed her dreams ~ more than what most people do in a lifetime. She wanted to leave a legacy for her children while helping other young women in domestic situations. Her life and her legacy will do just that. It is my belief that her life ~ Her story, will SAVE other lives!

* * * * * * * * * * * * * * * * * * *

100% of Aliyah's agreed upon royalties earned will be placed into a fund for her children.

Jesus, Coffee, and Prayer Christian Publishing House will make sure of this!

May this Queen REST in HEAVENLY PEACE

* * * * * * * * * * * * * * * * * * *

~Note from the Publisher~

Love Doesn't HURT

Domestic Violence Is NEVER Okay

If you or someone you love needs help

Please Call the National Domestic Violence Hotline @1.800.799.SAFE (7233)

* * * * * * * * * * * * * * * * * * *

Strength to the powerless

By: Dr. Radisha Brown

"He gives power to the weak and strength to the powerless."
NLT Isaiah 40:29

Known as 'The Wellogist,' I am the Founder and CEO of Holistic Living with Dr. Radisha. I provide practical tips and encouragement to help women overcome depression, emotional pain, and traumatic experiences; if left unchecked, trauma leads to unhealthy weight gain. My desire to support women has led to my #1 Bestselling book "Girl Get Off the Couch" – Stop the self- hate and lose the weight. I utilize not only my professional experience as a licensed therapist but incorporate my personal struggles and experience of using food to cope with emotional pain.

The journey to becoming a self-confident and powerful Queen, did not happen overnight. My personal journey was filled with emotional and physical challenges such as depression and obesity. My journey – to get past perceived setbacks and what felt like an impossible past.

There is a huge difference between impossible and difficult!

Powerless to change

My longtime friends remember "Big Radisha." New friends are always in disbelief when I show them pictures of a 200+ pounds me. They always tell me "that's not you!" However, my longtime friends were there and remember loving me through my worst times. They remember me spending days and nights on my couch eating and sleeping my life away.

It was time for "Big Radisha" to GO and "Healthy Radisha" to start LIVING!

At the height of my depression, my body was in constant physical and emotional pain.

I felt Hopeless. Worthless. Lonely. **My body was circling its own rock bottom, desperate for love and attention.** My body's pain was like an emergency siren going off. In response, I did what my body was calling out for and I went to the doctor. Deep down inside, I knew it was time to see the doctor for help; but, I was in fear of what was coming -Shame.

I remember sitting on the table when my doctor came in to discuss my lab results. I could barely move. I was paralyzed with the pain and weight of my depression. He reviewed my results briskly, aggressively, and with a matter of fact no-nonsense demeanor. He said four words that I will Never forget. "You are too fat!" My mind immediately started to race. *'I mean, excuse me?' Too fat?! Who are you to just say that to me? How dare you? You don't know who I am, what I am going through or how I feel.* **But his words yelled out in my brain, "too fat, too fat, too fat!" His next words struck me down to my core, he asked me, "Do you want to live, or do you want to die?"** I thought to myself, what kind of words are these to say to someone who struggles with depression – someone who copes just to make it through the day? Of course, I wanted to live, but I didn't have the tools required to change

> ## "Change what you're doing or die."

He just said it so plainly, so rudely. My immediate response was to push back in anger. My defenses rose up instantly and I blurted out with righteous confidence, **"everybody doesn't have to be a size two."**

To be honest, I don't think he was used to patients speaking up and pushing back a bit. He just closed my lab work and walked out of the room, leaving me totally alone and marinating on the news that I was heading towards death. I sat there on the table, feeling the paper sheet beneath me, staring at the ceiling tiles, as I broke down and cried. This was my heaviest moment, my lowest moment. I had to listen to my body which was constantly in pain and crying out for care and attention. I felt broken and confused, I felt like I went to get the help my body asked for and this was the response?

I felt awful. Those nagging lies that depression tells you -crept all over me, I am worthless, hopeless, and helpless. In that moment I also got boiling mad. That stubborn fire flared up in me and I wanted to go back and find that doctor and let him know that he was *wrong*. I wanted to shove it in his face, prove to him that I did want to live, that I didn't want to die. But, before I could storm out and give him a piece of my mind, my saving grace entered the room.

My Nurse came in a few minutes after the doctor left. She was immediately a *breath of fresh air*; she felt familiar, like we were from the same place. She had kind eyes and carried a small pack of tissues, which she immediately shared with me. As I sat there crying, she consoled me, she apologized for the behavior of the doctor, explained that he was a difficult man who was inappropriate at times. She made it clear to me that he was in the wrong with his behavior, that there were other ways of communicating with patients. I was floored, that this stranger just immediately took my side, **made me feel seen** and heard without me saying a word.

My Inner Power

My nurse offered words of encouragement that changed my life. She gently rested a hand on my shoulder and let me know that I could get better by making **small changes**. I had never thought of it like that before – everything I wanted always felt so big, so far away and unattainable so why even try? *But small changes, I could do those.*

I left that doctor's office and called my friends to tell them about my experience at the doctor's office. They answered the call and shared in my pain and anger. They got mad with me; they validated that anger in a structured way that encouraged me to move past it and onto the bigger issue at large – my depression. Most of all, my sister held my hand through this time; she gave me the encouragement I needed to feel loved, seen, and supported. My body was crying out for help, not just because I was pushing it toward death, but because I was depressed. That big culprit, the worst bad guy – depression. Food was just my coping mechanism – my way of self-medicating.

> Some people use alcohol or pills, but I used food.

Support where it counts

The key for losing weight and loving myself the way I deserved was in dealing with my depression. Through the love and support of my friends and sister, I found my personal therapist and began my journey to who I am today. With this loving support system, I was able to change my own mind – the first step to loving the person I truly am. I started to recognize that I have unique gifts and talents. I learned my self-worth.

Q.U.E.E.N Tip

> I am Valuable Queen and so are you!

I thank God for the nurse who came in with that first little nugget of encouragement; who saw me at my lowest and inspired me to start small. I thank God for my sister and all my friends who held up the mirror of true love that reflects the truth:

> I have value…
>
> I am worth the effort and energy…
>
> I am worth the investment
>
> ***and the world needs me!***

I am so thankful for these friends and loved ones. I am so thankful and honored to help other women suffering from depression and an unhealthy weight. Helping Queens discover how to love themselves, mind, body, and soul is what I've been called to do!

NOW

I am equally thankful that I answered my body's call for real help because **I can share a way out with others.** Once I started this journey it set me on a wonderful path. Not just a path of self-love and acceptance, but one of sharing this gift with others. Sharing my personal journey allows me to equip others with essential tools to finding their very own self-worth and value.

Q.U.E.E.N Tips

You are more powerful than you know. You hold the keys to sparking someone else's desire to find true self-worth.

- Daily affirmations are short, powerful, yet simple statements designed to manifest a specific goal. Start each day with a positive affirmation which can be as simple as "I am healthy", or "I am worthy".

- So, Queen, ***NEVER*** Give Up- ***REACH*** for your friends and family and ***SEEK*** help when you know it's time.

About the Author

Dr. Radisha Brown is a serial entrepreneur, transformative speaker, licensed therapist, and author of the #1 Best-Selling book "Girl Get Off the Couch". Dr. Brown is the host of Therapy Matters Radio Show where stories of triumph are shared along with tips on how you can overcome your greatest struggles with holistic living and tackling the source of your depression. Her passion and mission in life is to inspire others to dream, achieve and overcome any challenges. You can listen to Therapy Matters weeknights at 9PM on WDJY 99.1FM in Atlanta, Georgia.

Connect with this Queen via

- **Website:** https://www.drradisha.com/
- **Phone:** 833-825-5285
- **Email:** info@drradisha.com
- **Instagram:** https://www.instagram.com/drradishabrown/
- **Facebook:** https://facebook.com/drradishabrown

* * * * * * * * * * * * * * * * *

Purpose Produces Promise

By: Ja'nae Sturgis

"But you, God, see the trouble of the afflicted; you consider their grief and take it in hand. The victims commit themselves to you; you are the helper of the fatherless. Psalm 10:14 NIV

The Excuse

In my walk with God, I have been through a series of events in life that left me with more questions than answers. The human mind could not comprehend the level of the attacks from the enemy; attacks designed to abort my purpose, snatch my identity and destroy my destiny, starting at a very early age. I was sexually abused at the age of nine and struggled carrying this deep dark secret in my heart; I found the courage to break my silence in my early thirties. Over the course of thirty years, my spirit was vulnerable to the vices of the enemy; I had unknowingly allowed the enemy full access to reign over my thoughts and my actions. This opened the door to other contaminated spirits that attached themselves to me and I later learned how they would manifest. I went from being a sweet, innocent, loving little girl with dreams and aspirations of becoming an African-American Historian, to a grown woman who still had not fully healed from the scars and wounds of the sexual abuse.

Looking back on my young adult years, my challenge was always establishing and maintaining healthy relationships. I found myself participating in a perpetual cycle of toxic behaviors, settling for less than I deserved, unaware of my value and lacking self-worth. My heart was full of anger, rage, bitterness, resentment, pride, fear, rejection and abandonment. Unaware of my identity in Christ at the time, I allowed people, situations and circumstances to define me as an individual. So I settled for men who were just as broken as I, feeling unworthy of love.

I was empty on the inside and constantly looking to drown my sorrows; I suppressed pain that I had been harboring for years. Although I was in relationships, I still felt lonely and gave practically no thought to who I was letting into my intimate space. I would later learn that Jesus is the only one who can permanently fill this emptiness. According to John 6:35 NIV, Jesus said, "I am the bread of life. He who comes to Me shall never hunger, and he who believes in Me shall never thirst."

> Time after time, I allowed men with dirty hands to contaminate my heart and spirit.

Initially, my relationships started out perfect; they would shower me with all kinds of gifts, compliments and even engagement rings. Before I knew it, I was falling right back into the enemy's trap. I suffered a miscarriage due to emotional and physical abuse which led to deep depression. I often *entertained thoughts of suicide* to escape the pain. No one knew just how bad things had gotten for me though friends could sense that something was not right. I was infamous for isolating myself to avoid facing the pain.

I wanted to break this demonic self-sabotaging cycle. Eventually came the realization that I could not do it in my own strength, **but**

I needed God to intervene.

I remember saying repeatedly, "God, I've already tried to do it my way and things progressively got worse; so at this point, I give it all over to you." Slowly but surely, I decided to place my trust in the Master's hands. Little by little, I began praying to the Lord for guidance and deliverance. He led me to a few foundational scriptures to reflect on my identity in Him.

I meditated on some key scriptures until they became seeds planted in my spirit that would bear good fruit.

- **1 Peter 2:9 NIV** "But you are a chosen people, a royal priesthood, a holy nation, God's special possession, that you may declare the praises of him who called you out of darkness into his wonderful light."
- **Colossians 3:1-3 NIV** "Since, then, you have been raised with Christ, set your hearts on things above, where Christ is, seated at the right hand of God. Set your minds

on things above, not on earthly things. For you died, and your life is now hidden with Christ in God.

- **2 Corinthians 5:17 NKJV** "Therefore, if anyone is in Christ, he is a new creation; old things have passed away; behold, all things have become new."

- **Philippians 2:5 KJV** "Let this mind be in you, which is also in Christ Jesus."

Once I was able to identify who I was in Him, He then led me to scriptural references concerning matters of my heart. At this point, I realized that God is a God of order, and that His thoughts are not my thoughts, and His ways are not my ways.

- **1 Samuel 16:7 NIV** "The Lord doesn't see things the way you see them. People judge by outward appearance, but The Lord looks at the heart."

- **Psalm 51:10 KJV** "Create in me a clean heart, O God; and renew a right spirit within me."

- **Ezekiel 36:26 NIV** "I will give you a new heart and put a new spirit in you; I will remove from you your heart of stone and give you a heart of flesh."

The more time I spent meditating on His Word and in His presence, the more I began to understand what it really means to surrender and *yield* myself to HIS will for my life.

After twenty one days of fasting and prayer, I could tell that He was cleaning me up on the inside. I no longer had a desire to pursue or entertain meaningless relationships. Instead, I made the conscious decision to focus on God, walk in authority, watch the posture of my heart, love His people and take my Royal Position as a joint heir of Christ.

> God took the very process that the enemy tried to use to destroy me and turned it into a Kingdom assignment!

Kingdom Assignment

I had no idea that God had plans to use me in the very area in which I struggled. I found that I had a gift of encouragement, a desire to inspire women, and a burden to help those who found themselves in similar *toxic cycles of abuse*. In 2018, The Lord gave me a vision with instructions to lay the groundwork for a non-profit organization geared towards restoring women to their rightful positions in God. In addition, The Lord allotted me opportunities to share my testimony on blog sites, at women conferences and in small intimate settings. I spent time interceding for women, crying with women, and decreeing the Word of The Lord over their futures, and their destinies.

I am a firm believer that process produces pain, pain produces power, power produces purpose, and purpose produces promise.

Supporting Cast

I am a firm believer that God shows us just how much He loves by the covenant relationships He chooses for us. When I think about the people sent to me by God, I have no words to express how much they mean to me. They cover me in prayer, they encourage me, they impart wisdom, they rebuke me when necessary, they believe in me, and they lift up my hands when I feel like I cannot go any further. They challenge me, they strengthen me, and they love me unconditionally. We laugh together, cry together, worship together, pray together, and support one another's business and ministry endeavors. In many ways, these women reflect me because we all share similar testimonies. I trust that they hear from the Lord and humbly welcome their valuable feedback as I continue to press toward the mark for the prize of the high calling.

My Winning Team

When the Lord gave me the vision to start planning the details for non-profit, I shared the idea with the women in my circle. Right away, they became ecstatic about the positive impact this program would have on women in the area. Without hesitation, some began conducting research and making phone calls, some provided insight and wisdom based on experience with non-profits, and others prayed that the vision would come to pass at the appointed time. As a circle, we make time weekly for check-ins and prayer sessions to share the progress of our ministry assignments and business endeavors.

In my overall experience in dealing with toxic people and meaningless relationships, I've learned that when people are sent by God, you will see the manifestation of His fruit. Proverbs 27:17 NIV, reminds us "As iron sharpens iron, so one person sharpens another." If you are not discerning, the enemy will send people with ulterior motives to cause strife, confusion and to sow discord. Your covenant circle should always be a representation of your relationship with Christ.

Q.U.E.E.N Tip

If ever in doubt, pray for wisdom and discernment and allow the Lord to guide you.

Now

While growing in maturity and intimacy with the Christ, I was able to understand the sensitivity of His perfect timing – not moving ahead of God and not lagging. 2 Timothy 4:2 NKJV tells us that we are to be ready both in season and out of season.

Q.U.E.E.N Tip

If you ever find yourself in a holding pattern, keep praying and worshipping, keep serving, and keep seeking His face. Allow Him to keep developing you; so when He opens the door, you are prepared to take your Royal Position.

About the Author

Ja'nae Sturgis is a woman of God with a heart geared towards helping and encouraging His people. She has a very meek and humble spirit and is devoted to her calling to serve in Ministry.

A Business Woman, Domestic Violence Survivor, a Conference Speaker, a Mentor, and an Intercessor, Ja'nae has connected with and poured into people from all walks of life.

She also has a passion for motivating; inspiring and helping future entrepreneurs turn their dreams into reality and firmly believes in the formula "Process>Pain>Power>Purpose>Promise."

* * * * * * * * * * * * * * * * * * *

It Hurts like Hell

By: Tamika Morrow

"Brothers and sisters, I do not consider myself yet to have taken hold of it. But one thing I do: Forgetting what is behind and straining toward what is ahead. I press on toward the goal to win the prize for which God has called me heavenward in Christ Jesus."

Philippines 3:13-14

Powerful Excuses

My excuses were **Powerful** enough to make me a prisoner to my own procrastination for years. Often struggling to mentally cope with everyday life problems had turned me into a depressed version of myself – a self that I didn't recognize. Family and friends were clueless.

The Purpose

I always knew that God had a greater purpose for my life. I was created to minister the *Word of God to His people through music*. But before I could truly walk in the path of my calling, my faith in God would be tested. *I was emotionally weak and spiritually malnourished.* My own doubts and fears were steadily destroying my own potential and *I was getting in my own way.* Emotional outbursts were a daily part of my routine, especially when I was at my weakest. Negative thoughts would take precedent over any positive thought that would try to bloom in my mind. So much so, that I would discredit anyone who had the audacity to speak positivity over me.

Negativity is Real

My decisions, partnered with spiritual attacks, almost stopped me from prospering.

A heavy dose of depression and insecurities resulted in my spiritual gates being left unguarded. The war on my mental and spiritual wellbeing was raging.

The Realization

At that point, I realized that if there was anything wrong in my life, I was to blame. The time to stop making excuses had come. In that darkest period of my life, I lost meaningful relationships with family and friends. Sometimes, you must lose before you gain – that includes relationships. God took me on a spiritual journey that tested my faith, *relentlessly* pushed me out of my comfort zone, and ultimately brought me closer to Him.

It Hurts like Hell

One on one time with my Father drew me nearer to Him and away from peers and so-called family and friends. My isolation period lasted for months but felt like eternity – it hurt like hell. Winston Churchill said, "If you're going through hell, keep going." Although there were many lonely nights in the flesh, God was setting me up to experience the full measure of His love and goodness for me. A deeper understanding was revealed to me when I cried and sobbed my heart out to Him. Heartfelt talks and regular prayer became my new normal. In hindsight, I now understand that although I was strong willed in many areas, I was just as weak spiritually in many others. When the Calling over your life is GREAT, even a strong-willed woman will run into adversity while on her quest. My determination and strong will lead to misunderstandings and breakdowns that only ***God would be able to fix.***

God intentionally had to snatch me out of my comfort zone to produce greatness. Without God's precision pressure points, I would have never been prompted to move on my own. To become the strong woman that you see today, walking in her purpose, I had to endure great hardship and adversity. Now I understand why.

> ## How can I effectively minister to God's people if I had never been tested?

God needed me isolated, in a place of vulnerability, seeking Him alone in prayer to transform my life and thus transform the lives of those connected to me. ***I became a stronger woman when my life was POWERED by the living Word of God!***

Supporting Cast

To be perfectly honest, as I reflected on my journey to a better me, I realized that it was extremely hard for me to communicate my needs when I was in survival mode. When my life was falling apart, I was uncertain, embarrassed, and in a state of shock. God allowed me to fall from my perceived mountain top in front of His people. I had to hit rock bottom to fully understand His *grace* and love for me. I was in the process of losing everything that meant the most to me and the reason was very clear. There were many issues that I needed to come to grips with before I could truly emerge into the strong purpose-filled woman God was calling me to be. Immediately after I touched rock bottom I looked at my surroundings. In my state of embarrassment, I wanted to see who else was right there with me. God reveals all.

Q.U.E.E.N Tip

You never know who your true friends are until life throws you a curveball.

I had humbled myself to reach out to friends and family that I thought would help me in my time of need. I was stricken to find out that they were not there. I felt resentment. While I was at my lowest, only a few tried and true friends stepped forward to be by my side during my test – a season of failure and consequences. My husband, who continued to be my anchor and rock, responded to the call along with other peers who I had not expected to aid me. I believe that every person that was present in my life during those times were handpicked by God. Not only did they help me, but they taught me valuable lessons.

God Provides

The road to a better me has not been an easy one, to say the least. As a matter of fact, I am still traveling on that long, dusty road today. I quickly realized that we must learn to accept our own role leading to the painful situations in our lives. You will grow wiser and stronger in this process, just like I did. In the eyes of many, I had fallen from grace. Many of those I had personally supported were nowhere to be found in my time of need.

> But God never gave up on me.

God is truly my biggest supporter, during the good and bad times – poor judgement and bad decision times too! With the love and support of my better half, who loves me unconditionally, God has made me victorious.

Moment of Reflection

The world can be cold and unforgiving – filled with hypocrites at times. But along my journey towards self-love, healing, and God's redemption, I have made a big discovery.

> I discovered that there is a bond that will link you to your true family and sometimes that bond is not of blood.

In my wilderness season, God clearly revealed to me who was truly a part of my support system.

Some people will never have the luxury of knowing who truly has their back. These people will spend their entire lives surrounded by people who do not truly love them. **I consider myself to be blessed.**

My Now

I am so thankful for where God has brought me to spiritually and mentally right now. During my wildness season of brokenness, God was laying the framework for my restoration in Him. I learned to rely on God and trust in His word. Like Paul, I have not yet arrived, but I am learning *how* to bloom wherever God decides to plant me. I NOW rejoice in the process to becoming a better me.

I often remind myself that who I am becoming is far more important than what anyone else thinks of me.

I have a great work to do; the work that I put in now will shape who I become in Him. My detour DID NOT erase nor eradicate my destiny, or the unique calling God has placed over my life. **God will always have the final say!**

Q.U.E.E.N TIP

Never allow fear to stop you from MOVING forward. Even if you fall on your face – know that you are still moving forward. Small steps will eventually turn into miles.

About the Author

Mika Morrow is a singer/ songwriter originally from Baltimore, Maryland. Born again and a bible believer, Mika is on a mission to impact lost souls who need guidance and healing in today's world through the ministry of song. In her early years she attended the Baltimore School for the Arts where she majored in voice. In addition to building a career as a professional background singer for various Award-winning Gospel Artists in the music ministry, she is a loving wife and mother of two. She recently released her new hit single called "Move" as her very first solo track. Her song is one of 2 themed songs for the Q.U.E.E.N Xperience platform.

Support this Queen

FB @TamikaMorrow

IG @MikaMorrow

www.mikamorrowmusic.com

* * * * * * * * * * * * * * * * *

The Secret
Purpose is your Birthright

By: Deborah Tulay

"And we know [with great confidence] that God [who is deeply concerned about us] causes all things to work together [as a plan] for good for those who love God, to those who are called according to His plan *and* purpose." Romans 8:28 AMP

You are a Queen full of potential, possibility, and power.

Before you were formed in the womb of your mother, God knew you. You have been birthed into purpose, on purpose. Purpose is the reason for which something was created and exists. It answers the "why" to your existence.

The journey to purpose begins before we are born, but is shaped by our childhood belief systems. I can personally attest that everything touching my life for many years had the residue of my past childhood beliefs. Belief systems are embedded between the ages of four and eight years of age. The events that happen during this time have the propensity to affect our lives for many years to come. My childhood presented life challenges that seared into the very fiber of my emotions and unapologetically wounded my soul.

Tap…tap… Tap, tap… Tap, tap… was a sound I often heard at night when lying in bed as a young child beside my mom in our modest four room, tin roof, wooden house – a living room, a kitchen, and two bedrooms. It's raining. As it rained outside, it also rained inside. The rain trickled, and at other times it poured, into the buckets placed strategically throughout the house to keep the floors dry. As I lie in bed with my arm around my mother, the deep fear that I felt momentarily subsided; it was replaced with a faint assurance that I was safe, and everything would be all right. I was the last child born to a single mom doing it all on her own. By the time I was born, she had been divorced for quite a few years. After years of domestic violence, she got out of a marriage and into vulnerable situations where she found herself looking for love in all the wrong faces.

During that era, it was not uncommon for men and women to be in intimate relationships with neighbors, friends, church members etc. and bring children into the world that were ***kept a secret.*** I was one of those children. I was born to a single mom of seven and a married Baptist pastor.

I was born a secret – a scandalous predicament, wrapped in a spirit of rejection, and fear that would have its hold on me for many years of my life.

The first several years of my life I thought that my sister and I shared the same father. Mr. Jim (as we affectionately called him) along with his family was nice to me, but different with her – more gifts more doting upon her. Hmmm. I often wondered why. My sister was often told in my presence that she was pretty and looked like my mother sharing mom's tan complexion and long thick black hair. But I, like my father, was dark-skinned and had block plats (short hair). I grew up believing that I was not good enough, pretty enough, or smart enough. That was my introduction to an inferiority complex and low self-esteem. These were companions to the fear and rejection that already gripped my mind. She's ok, but I am not ok.

Finding out the identity of my biological father, a pastor, generated feelings of hurt, betrayal, disappointment and shame. The rejection and fear amidst a scandal produced a soul wound in my life. A soul wound is not seen by the natural eye or I could have treated it, covered it, or provided an antibiotic ointment. But it is a wound that is deeply rooted inside of your soul realm and affects thought and response in every area of your life. The devil had a hit out on my purpose and knew that if he could distort my belief systems, he would be able to manipulate the trajectory of my life. But it is through our life challenges and the power of the Holy Spirit that our purpose can be ignited!

At the age of fifteen, I found myself, just like my mother, vulnerable and looking for love in all the wrong faces. I was seeking love, validation and affirmation that I never received from my father. I knew who he was, and he knew who I was, but we never had a relationship. Because of it I had an undisclosed Father Wound that plagued my life. By the time I was sixteen years old I gave birth to a beautiful baby girl. Life continued, tarnished by the Father Wound. At twenty-five, I had a fairy tale wedding while still looking for love in all the wrong faces. Before marriage, he seemed to be an awesome protector, provider, disciplinarian, and a counselor (hmmm…characteristics of a father). I unknowingly, subconsciously was seeking a father and not a husband. I was expecting my husband to fill a role that was not his responsibility to fill. He had his own issues along with my need to be fathered. Following many years of domestic violence from a perverted father role, I got the courage to get out and get a divorce. I felt fearful, rejected, and broken. Unbeknownst to me at the time was a hidden culprit. Only God could fill the void and heal my Father Wound.

In 2012, I was diagnosed with breast cancer. It was through this journey that God opened my eyes to my Royal Position as a Spiritual Purpose Navigator. Life is like a vapor; we can be here one moment and gone the next. I adopted Romans 8:28 along with the words "Living Life on Purpose" as my life mantra. I began blogging and wrote my first book, "Grace for The Journey".

The Excuse

I was awake and hungry for change, but I didn't know what the next steps were. I finally overcame my fear and **QUIT** my excuses. I got out of my own way, stepped out on faith, and hired a coach. My coach taught me self-love, the importance of self-discovery, the process of deep diving, and excavation to find the root. As I did the work, God began to reveal my worth and showed me the root of my issues – a Father Wound. After receiving revelation and healing, (it's a process), the residue from that old belief system began to fade away.

Understanding

We all catch glimpses of our destiny along our journey. I have always had a love for helping people, especially hurting women. God knows who we are and the potential that lies on the inside of us. I now

UNDERSTAND that my assignment is to support women that struggle with purpose blockage. I help her to move beyond fear, doubt, and self-sabotage to release her passion, power, and potential and walk in her destiny. The ladies that surround me or **ENLISTED** in this work I call "Grace Girls". They are an *Established* godsend and help to plan and execute all Life on Purpose events. I cannot do it alone.

Queen always remember, everything you will ever be is in you at the time that God formed you – while you were in your mother's womb.

Low self-esteem, low self-worth, lack of confidence, and soul level wounds will work hand in hand to keep you from seeing yourself the way that God sees you. It's a tactic of the enemy to keep you from taking your Royal Position. Keep in mind that **you are fearfully and wonderfully made** in God's image and in his likeness. Everything about you is exactly the way that the Father has intended. Regardless of what anyone says, thinks, or does, it is important that you believe what God says about you! People are waiting on you to get in position. They need you. Playing your Royal Position will require you to patiently navigate life and allow your passion to lead you into your God-ordained purpose. You may not know all the answers, but trust the process. Purpose will receive its legitimacy through your passionate responses to experiences. It is through our trust and release that we allow God to take every moment and use it for His glory until it works together for our good. It's not always easy, but it's always worth it!

It doesn't matter where you are in life right now or what you have been through, you have an assignment – a Royal Position to fulfill. Don't allow history to assassinate your destiny! Thoughts of your past often create negative energy. Take authority over every non-productive, purpose robbing, disillusioned thought; render it harmless and cast it down!

Q.U.E.E.N TIP

> Live life full out and on purpose even if you must do it scared!

I know what that feels like and I encourage you to press through! If you don't do something, nothing will ever happen. God will bless what we do. Queen take your place, walk in your Royal Position and do it **NOW!** Love yourself in a Life On Purpose!

About the Author

Deborah Tulay is the International speaker and Best-Selling Co-author of 'Fear to Freedom'. She is an ordained Minister, Elder of her church, a seven-year breast cancer survivor, and domestic violence survivor. She is a radio personality, spiritual navigator, and the CEO & Founder of Pink Treasures.

Connect with this Queen:

FB @DeborahTulay

IG @debtulaylifeonpurpose

www.dtulayonpurpose.com

* * * * * * * * * * * * * * * * *

Trusting His Voice

By: Sherry Jones

"Your own ears will hear him. Right behind you a voice will say,
"This is the way you should go," whether to the right or to the left."
Isaiah 30:21 NLT

It took me ten years to release my first book! Not because I lacked the talent and resources to complete it. Not because I didn't have the support of family and friends. It took me ten long years because I didn't trust what God told me. I allowed fear and insecurity to block my blessing.

Quit Making Excuses

*I*n 2006, I was active in my church and utilized my skills as a writer to assist with the church newsletter and write/direct plays for the youth ministry. I was excited to glorify God through my work. Everything was going well until one of my plays was misunderstood. I was told it wasn't anointed or God-inspired. I was devastated because I believed it was the story He wanted me to share. I became unsure of my gift and my ability to clearly hear from God. Was He using me like I thought He was? Was I qualified to work in ministry?

Despite my insecurities, I was led to start writing my book in 2007. Unfortunately, I only completed a couple of chapters before I got stuck. I tried to redeem myself with another play, but it was canceled. Writing was no longer something I was proud of. It became a struggle and a cross to bear. I was in a spiritual valley, clamoring to get out. My husband and I left the church and my heartache prevented me from walking in my calling. My experience became my excuse not to write. It manifested as fear, procrastination, and lack of confidence. What if I wrote something else that wasn't Godly? What if the Church wouldn't accept what I had to offer?

I finally joined a new church in 2011, but the last thing I wanted to do was work in ministry or write. I resolved to be a pew sitter; enjoying service and going home without being involved. That didn't last for long. One of my friends exposed my hidden talents and I eventually started writing plays and working with the youth again. I worked on my book here and there but didn't make much progress.

I would tell people I was writing a book and it would be released soon, but soon never came. People started calling me on my bluff and asking about it. When was I going to finish it? What was I waiting on? I realized my calling was bigger than my excuses. There was a story that needed to be told and I was the vessel God chose to tell it. I had to trust Him and walk in it.

Understand Your Assignment

My assignment is to be a writer after God's own heart. I battled low self-esteem for most of my life. I never felt good enough, smart enough or pretty enough. It took decades for me to see myself through His eyes, not mine. Life experiences tried to beat me down, but His love was always there. I was able to share that message through my book. Although it's fiction, the main character's thoughts and feelings are based on my younger self and the evolution I experienced to become who I am today. I will continue to share my testimony and the power of God's love with future book projects. *Trouble Don't Last Always* is just the beginning!

Our testimonies are not for us. Allow your testimony to lead you to your assignment. He can use your good, bad and ugly to impact the hearts and minds of many.

Enlist Your Supporting Cast

I have a great family and a large group of friends and associates, **but my inner circle was the supporting cast I needed to realize my assignment**. They are three phenomenal women of God who are not afraid to tell me when I'm wrong, push me towards my goals and cheer for my accomplishments. They met me during different phases of my life and have different perspectives on my journey. One has known me since I was a child, another met me my sophomore year in college and the other met me in my late twenties.

It's great to have a supporting cast who really knows you and has a history with you. They are often see more in you than you see in yourself while being honest, wise and discerning. They are not "yes" men and women. They don't care if you get angry and huff and puff. They just want to share the truth in love. My supporting cast did all of that and more!

Establish Your Winning Team

Each member of my inner circle played a specific role in helping me complete my book.

One was the Enforcer. I asked her to help me set deadlines and keep me on task. She texted and called to check on my status. She pushed me, delivered tough love when needed and called me out on my tendency to self-sabotage and get distracted. I got frustrated and irritated, but she never let me falter.

One was the Creative Director. She's also a gifted writer and I asked her to be the content editor for my book. She told me the things that needed to be corrected, made suggestions for improvement and calmed me down when I started freaking out. She made sure my book was a professional, quality piece of art. I was difficult at times, but she stuck with me.

The last one was the Exhorter. I asked her to keep me motivated. She was always there with encouragement, a prophetic word and prayer to help me along the way. She constantly reminded me of how far I had come and why I needed to keep going. My confidence needed a boost at times and she always delivered.

I am blessed to have these wonderful women in my life. I wouldn't have made it without them.

Now

On August 23, 2017, my life changed forever. I will never forget the moment I clicked the submit button and *Trouble Don't Last Always* went live on Amazon. I felt the weight of my fears and insecurities lifted. There was no turning back. It was out there for the world to see. My worries were released in an instant – whether people would like it, if it was God-inspired, and whether it would be a flop or a success. Ten years of blood, sweat, tears, hopes, and dreams were manifested at that moment.

My dream of becoming a published author came true and my assignment was set in motion. I quit making excuses, understood my assignment, enlisted my supporting cast, established my winning team and acted now! I was a QUEEN playing my royal position and living my life according to God's rules, not mine. I trusted the process and it paid off. I'm now able to live in freedom. There's nothing better than that!

Q.U.E.E.N TIP

Trust your relationship with God and how He directs you. Don't let anyone cause you to doubt what you have been told. Walk in it and use your talents to glorify Him.

Q.U.E.E.N PRAYER

Dear Lord,

Thank you for your gifts, guidance, and direction. Help me to distinguish and listen to your voice. If you said it, I believe it. I will not allow the opinions of others to cause me to doubt the truth you have shared with me. Bless my mess and make it a message for you. In Jesus' name. Amen.

About the Author

Sherry Jones is an author and motivational speaker. Her novel *Trouble Don't Last Always,* is available for purchase on Amazon. Sherry's motto is "The power of life and death is in the tongue; choose life". She enjoys sharing her life experiences and empowering others to make that choice.

Connect with this Queen

FB @SherrySpeaksLife

IG @author_sherryjones

www.sherryspeakslife.com

* * * * * * * * * * * * * * * * * * *

Weight of Why I Worship

By: Evangelist Evonn Firms

"and provide for those who grieve in Zion – to bestow on them a crown of beauty instead of ashes, the oil of joy instead of mourning, and a garment of praise instead of a spirit of despair. They will be called oaks of righteousness, a planting of the LORD for the display of his splendor." Isaiah 61v.3 NIV"

"But they that wait upon the Lord shall renew their strength; they shall mount up with wings as eagles; they shall run, and not be weary; and they shall walk, and not faint." Isaiah 40v. 31 KJV

My focus scriptures are speaking to those of whom have found themselves in a place of waiting on the promises of God to manifest in their lives.

The waiting season can be discouraging to many; and I am no stranger to either the discouragement or the waiting season. However, these scriptures have truly encouraged me throughout those times.

Self-Constructed Walls of Defense

Walls can either help or hinder us. Many of us have built walls to protect us from being hurt again and have relied solely on this as a defense mechanism. I once heard an elder say that not only do walls keep the wrong things out; but walls also keeps us from allowing the right things in. I must admit that I learned from a very young age to never get too attached to anything or anyone. It was in my childhood that I developed the fear of not being in control of my own life. As I journeyed in life, I would not make any attempts to establish friendships or relationships with others. It was the crippling fear of avoiding mistakes. As the oldest child of my mother, I've always had high expectations placed upon me; hence that fear of failure has always found a way to locate me. This fear of not being able to know or trust what may or may not happen in a new marriage. So my ex-husband resurrected and re-erected my self-constructed walls of defense. Oh the walls have definitely kept me protected throughout the years; but the fear of failure hindered my walk as a believer. Christ began to reveal to me that my fear of failure was actually an act of not trusting God. The word clearly states in **Hebrews 11:6 we are told that without faith it is impossible to please God**. It is due to the conviction of this scripture that I can trust God with the outcome of everything in my life. With the key elements of discernment and wisdom, I began the demolition process of walls that were placing restrictions on me. The fear of the what-ifs and the unknown have become easier as I have learned that both fear and faith cannot live or reside within the walls of my heart. So as you read this today, this is in fact a result of that demolition process. **My voice outside of those self-constructed walls.**

Your Assignment

I have always had a protective spirit, mostly due to being an older sibling. I have always found myself defending others. I was the friend who could always bring opposing sides into agreement or at least suggest mutual respect and consideration be given. Both parties favored me. Wow the stories I could tell you of my school days and friendships. I *understood* early in life the power and significance of prayer by hearing and watching my grandmother pray; and of course I'm a 'preacher's kid times two". From an early age I've had dreams of things happening; and when those dreams manifested, I would feel very strange. As I got older I began to understand, that when I had particular visions and dreams, it was my responsibility to pray and intercede for others. It was from having visions and dreams that I understood how important my prayers were; I learned to hear clearly from God and what He was revealing to me. I understood the importance and the characteristics of a praying wife; especially when a spouse may be face challenges that require healing and deliverance. Understanding that, in times of intercession for others, I began to realize how overwhelming it can be. Sometimes you can just see the outcome of a situation if the person you are interceding for continues to do things their own way, or succumb to generational curses, or be influenced and deceived by the enemy. As a divorced mother, I understood that this stage in life was the time that God would heighten my senses, visions, and intercession. It was my protective and nurturing spirit that allowed me to be so sensitive to the Holy Spirit's leading. I knew how to minister individually and reach each person based on their needs.

Have You Considered You

Many people have been influential in my life and contributed to my vision of ministry and future business endeavors. I can honestly say, it has been my experience with divorce and single parenthood that served as a means for me to enlist myself as my supporting cast. When you heal in the areas of brokenness, you will tap into God's will and purpose for your life. That empowers you to make the necessary changes to get better, want better, and do better. So I enlisted myself to be my biggest cheerleader, to place the word of God in every area of my life. I needed His power. I learned to take all my pieces and give them to God. He knows what to do with them.

Accountability

Many of you today have experienced some type of relationship that has ended quite possibly on bad and or not the best terms. I always say that ships are meant to be mobile; they should transport somewhere. God sent me a true friend who was more like a sister. Through many years we remained the best of friends, transcending geographical locations. She fought a long battle with cancer. During those times of uncertainty with her health, she spent countless days ministering to me and encouraging me to let go of the fear of failure; she stayed on me about my writings and to release them. It was her belief that my words empowered her. She knew God had a plan for His word that I had hidden in my heart along with the talent for writing that I often hid for many years throughout school. My dearly beloved best friend lost her battle to cancer on December 17, 2016. She, along with my three children, my parents, and my siblings have been my supporting cast. Through this journey, I have learned that people who really love you will not allow you to sit on your gifts; they will hold you accountable. There's so much untapped potential within you ladies. Don't be afraid to shine!

For Such a Time As This

For some of us it has taken of years of letting go and releasing our past issues with shame, making a conscious decision not to dummy down my anointing in this hour and this season; God's timing is perfect. My audience, like my calling, was already preselected.

Q.U.E.E.N TIP

It Was Good That You Were Afflicted

Believe that God can and will turn everything that the enemy meant for evil to your good. Put on your garment of praise and wear it daily. Praise can set the tone for your life; a garment can't be worn without putting it on! Work while you wait and remember praise is a choice!

Q.U.E.E.N PRAYER

Lord it is my prayer that every reader release brokenness, shame and fear unto You. Allow the spirit of forgiveness to permeate their whole being and grant them the fortitude and the strength to endure. Lord I pray that you bring total restoration to their lives in exchange for every tear they cried and every pain they bore. You will give them new garments of praise and beauty for ashes. Amen.

About the Author

Evonn Firms a proud mother of three who attained two Bachelor's degrees while being a divorced single mother. She is a licensed and ordained evangelist who has a heart and a burden for single mothers. She is the visionary and founder of two upcoming non-profit organizations Latter Rain Project and Sister Keepers Ministry.

Email: latterainmovement@gmail.com

Facebook: The Latter Rain Project and Sister Keepers Ministry

Instagram: evrenee31

Twitter: @Mpowrd2Nspire

* * * * * * * * * * * * * * * * * * *

Brittney Spears and Rock Bottoms

By: Dominique Burleson

"Many are the plans in the mind of a man, but it is the purpose of the LORD that will stand." Proverbs 19:21

Rock Bottom

We older millennials can certainly conjure up images of Britney circa 2007, Double Downs from KFC, Michael Jordan's baseball career, Crystal Pepsi, and George Clooney as Batman when considering some awful rock bottoms. These are things you just can't come back from, right?

If we look at all these "Rock Bottoms", we can see each person/company redeemed themselves, eventually. Heck, Generation Z was in elementary school when Britney decided to shave her head and take up umbrella sword fighting has no earthly idea what a Double Down is! It is a sandwich made with two chicken breasts instead of bread. Yeah. Now you're informed and grossed out. Now,

I know what you're saying. These aren't the kind of failures or hardships you're facing right now. These are a little extreme and, let's face it, celebs get away with a lot worse in the failure department. We give them a heck of lot more grace than the average person.

I get it. I do. In fact, I've had a TON of those not fun kind of rock bottoms. The ones that wouldn't make a decent meme and that I don't look back and chuckle at. In my marriage, my business, my finances, and in plenty of relationships – including mine with the Lord – I've face planted. A lot. However, when looking back, I can see how these experiences were just giving birth to something incredible. It just took a while. Let me take you back a bit.

In 2017, I started the business (after MANY failed businesses in various niches) I am currently in. I'm a digital marketing and brand consultant and I also run a lifestyle blog. This idea of helping business owners with their marketing stemmed from a friend asking for help. She saw how I managed my own social media presences over the years, and thought maybe I'd be able to help her out. This turned into my first real client. Man, was I pumped! I was finally figuring this thing out which meant we were on our way to being able to purchase a home – my ultimate goal.

My business began to take off a little. I was managing a small business owner's social media, I was teaching classes, I was even counseling other business owners. I had a fancy website and business cards. However, I was barely making enough money to pay for my expenses. I never took a day off. I was pretty much on call 24/7 willing to do anything and everything anyone ever wanted or needed. I was *constantly* asked to lower my prices, so I did. I did a $500 mini website design and setup for $75, only for the client to never get back with me. I was doing two and three hour seminars around the state for pennies. ***This led to being unsure of my worth and doubting my abilities. I began to barter.*** Some of this was successful, and some of it was not. I was having to work with our household income to pay for things I needed. Did I mention I'm a homeschooling mother of five? Yeah. I had a lot on my plate. Oh and if that wasn't enough, I missed writing. So I started a blog on my business site.

As you can probably tell, things began to get ugly. My relationship with my husband was starting to get exceptionally strained. I was neglecting my kids' schooling – something I swore I wouldn't allow to slip when taking on this job. I wasn't sleeping and I couldn't blame it on the nursing baby since I worked while he slept. Life was miserable. Truly, miserable. Then it happened. I snapped. Not just with an emotional response, but I really just broke. I blew up at my husband over something *obviously* unimportant because I can't remember it and I collapsed – in front of my babies. As I laid there on the floor with my children looking on in fright, my husband sat beside me. He rubbed my back and said, "Babe, this is killing you."

This is not what my dream was supposed to look like. I didn't understand how I could not live up this version of a #MomBoss I had in my head. Why could I not get ahead? Why was I not making money? Why, after an entire year, was I worse off than I was when I started? So I told a friend that I was going to quit all of it. Her response? "That's okay. It's okay to just be a mom. This [business] isn't for everyone." The disappointment was real. I ugly cried. I thought for sure I was going to get a quick kick in the butt, and some tough love. I was expecting, "This is what you were made for, but you need to figure out your priorities." Instead, I was encouraged to quit. Then, I told my husband. Anytime I got burned out with all my other business attempts, he was indifferent or just not invested at all, but I still told him. This time? His response was kind and compassionate. **He kneeled at my feet, took my hands, and said, "I'm sorry I never encouraged you in the past.** I'm sorry I always looked at the money part and never saw how great you are at this. But now, I'm telling you that you can't quit. She is wrong, and you're not 'just a mom'. This is what you're made for and I'll help you every step of the way." Y'all, this is my very introverted husband saying this to me. After eleven years, in that moment, he made me fall in love with him all over again. It was the most unexpected response I had heard. That was the moment that changed it all for me. This was my "put on your big girl panties" moment. I had my support. My love tank was full and I felt like I could conquer it all.

Now, are you thinking that I just went into overdrive and my business blew up? Nope. Quite the opposite. ***I walked away from EVERYTHING for three months.*** All my clients. All my social media. Even my blogs. Instead, I focused on my priorities – My Lord, my home, my husband, my kids, their education, and mine. I started taking classes and expanding my knowledge of business and my field. Then, the Lord began slowly opening up doors. One by one, I would sit in awe over how things would just "work out". Of course, the enemy would come in and try and mess things up at times, but opportunities were coming. Two steps forward one step back is still forward motion.

I now work on my terms. My business revolves around my life and not the other way around. I don't take everything I'm offered simply because it's a paid gig. Not every good thing is beneficial. Each thing I take on better be worth me being away from my family. That's a high bar, but it keeps me grounded. Because of the knowledge and experience I gained from hitting that rock bottom, literally, I wouldn't change things. And you best believe my husband reminds me of that day when I start taking a bunch of "good things" on again.

Now, dear friend, listen to me. You might be in the middle of your own rock bottom. You might be looking up from the pit wondering where He is in all of this. *Maybe your circle is doubting you.* Maybe the enemy is using others to make you doubt yourself. Maybe you have no clue of your value or worth. Maybe you're wanting to walk away from it all. **My advice to you:** Step back and run – don't walk – into the arms of the Father. Figure out YOU before you make another decision in your business. My problem was allowing the fear of missing opportunities to consume every decision. **Know what your true identity is and what your limits are. You were created with a purpose, but that purpose should not be an idol. It cannot rule you. In everything, line it up with your "why" and the Word. If it doesn't match up, you do not welcome it into your life.**

Proverbs 19:21 "Many are the plans in the mind of a man, but it is the purpose of the **LORD** that will stand."

About the Author

Dominique "DJ" Burleson is a delighted wifey and homeschooling mama to five little ones who resides in a little town outside of Charlotte, NC. She considers herself a storyteller, helping other mom bosses learn how to brand their own stories through marketing and blogging. She might consider sprinkled donuts her kryptonite, but she's certain Jesus would have put sprinkles and icing on his bread too.

Connect with this Queen

IG @djburleson

Blogs: http://www.djburleson.com

http://www.thebookishden.com

* * * * * * * * * * * * * * * *

Ripple Effect

By: Ashley Moraru

"The end of all things is near. Therefore be alert and of sober mind so that you may pray." 1 Peter 4:7-8

"Above all, love each other deeply, because love covers over a multitude of sins."

Everything we do right now ripples outward and affects everyone.

Our posture can shine our hearts or transmit anxiety. Our breath can radiate love or muddy the room in depression. Our glance can awaken joy. Our words can inspire freedom. Our every act can open hearts and minds. We all have our own royal positions that God has blessed us with and our responsibility as his children is to discover it, act upon it, and share it. For some it becomes clear at adulthood, for others at a young age. It really boils down to our attitude and acceptance.

Everyone has a story. Mine truly started at age seven when my parents got a divorce. Love was no longer a word I could believe in. My father, who cheated, lied, and then years later abused me physically and emotionally, has been the best and worst thing that has ever happened to me. Did he make my mother stronger by cheating? No, due to the overwhelming stress she had a heart attack and lost her personality. Did he make me stronger? Indeed, I had to be for myself, my now handicapped mother, and my siblings. I'm a big believer in the golden rule; treat others the way you want to be treated. It was the pain that made me decide to treat others with so much love that they wouldn't have room for discomfort. I acknowledge it is difficult to forgive a perpetrator for their wrongdoing; it goes against our moral code. Yet, if you consider it from a greater perspective, forgiveness is associated with your emotional welfare, not merely granting the other person pardon. I was able to accept what happened, forgive, and simply move on. This was a skill I learned at a young age and it opened many doors for me since I wasn't stuck in the past. I could have made up many excuses to not continue with life, or to have a sour outlook toward life, but I didn't. That alone was a blessing from God. I had an early understanding that He is always there, just like in the Footprint prayer.

I now have an attitude of taking one day at a time, keeping my head up high, and living life like God would want me too. I choose to be around people who I can grow from spiritually, knowing that would be the only way out of the pain. Do not except humans to make us whole, because only the Lord can grant us such peace. Yet again, we need to keep our hearts open, for God will place a man and or woman in our lives to help us with the trials. As so he rewarded me with my husband.

I met Serge Moraru at age sixteen; he was raised in a Christian household with two younger brothers and sisters. He was brought up with an abundant amount of love, major responsibilities, and little money. So he cultivated an old soul of appreciation and knowledge of life. God gave me the gift of his friendship and he is my treasure after all the pain. The plan I gave myself was to travel around the world working sales and meet as many people as I could. God had a different plan. He probably knew that I wouldn't have lasted long mentally without someone special to motivate me and point me in the right direction. Serge has saved my life multiple times. I will admit, even if I had my positive outlook in life I also had very dark times where I didn't see anything but darkness and sorrow. This is when Serge and my family would share their light and strength to keep me going. My grandparents are also my angels who looked after me, my sister, and my mother. They are the definition of unconditional love. The amount of time, love, and patience they gave to our future is immeasurable. I learned a lot of life lessons from them and became a well-rounded entrepreneur.

I would often sabotage myself because I was scared to be happy or thought I didn't deserve the success. Then I'd remember that, if our mentality screams madness, unacceptance, and unwillingness, we will only be in misery. What is a life without hope and faith? Why would we put ourselves in such a dark place of despair? I know that it is very easy to stay and hide in a state of depression. I have to remind myself that God blessed me with an ability to push myself and others in a peaceful direction. I break my bad habits and excuses by getting myself outside around others and sharing my royal position. Enjoy the art of conversation and giving back. The bible says to treat others the way you want to be treated and I took that as my goal to share with others. The secret is to put a smile on our face and try to radiate good vibes so others around us can sense an energy of love and compassion. Guiding others to work together to improve themselves and their communities can bring us much pride and joy!

Q.U.E.E.N Tip

Your positive attitude and everlasting faith can carry you in a more peaceful journey. Have faith that there is a bigger picture and know that your attitude can be felt by others. Spread your light and royal position in the world.

About the Author

Ashley Moraru is a child a God who enjoys helping others find peace in their journey. She loves making a hard situation into a smooth one, like a Real Estate transaction. She's been in sales her entire life and grew to understand the reason behind it. She loves to serve and takes much pride in doing so. She's also loved by her husband and two poodles.

Connect with this Queen

www.facebook.com/AshleyMoraruRealtor

www.instagram.com/charlotte_real_estate_agent/

www.twitter.com/1charlotteagent

www.linkedin.com/in/ashley-moraru-1a588545/

www.pinterest.com/CharlotteAgentAM/

* * * * * * * * * * * * * * * * *

The Reason to Get Ready

By: Tee Pringle

"And we know that in all things God works for the good of those who love him, who have been called according to his purpose." Romans 8:28 NIV

"For I know the plans I have for you," declares the Lord, "plans to prosper you and not to harm you, plans to give you hope and a future" Jeremiah 29:11 NIV

Purpose! A word that can look and mean something different to each person.

However, according to dictionary.com it means the reason for which something is done or created or for which something exists. The REASON something exists, just let that sink in. I love words so let's look at the word reason. Reason means a cause, explanation, or justification for an action or event. So, this word purpose is huge. Many people are searching for it, and very few find it. The thing about purpose to is that it is unique for every individual. God created you with a purpose in mind. YES YOU! Before he formed you in your mother's womb, He called you for His unique purpose. I believe that because there is a lack of purpose in our world today, people are just doing things aimlessly and there is a lack of fulfillment. And I don't mean doing things because of how we want other people to see us; I mean having an impact on someone's life because we are in the lane that God placed us. In our society there is so much self-centered behavior that we are missing the point of "securing the bag" or "making it". It's to better our lives yes, but also the lives of others. I solely believe that operating in purpose for real will always be "other people" centered. In this chapter I am going to share with you how finding my purpose has shaped this small town former foster child who lived in the projects into this confident woman I am today. Trust me, I have a long way to go but one thing is for sure; I know what and who I am and who God made me to be.

When I was 12 years old, my brothers and I were taken from my mom and placed in foster care.

Even before going into foster care I struggled with low self-esteem, depression, and fear. By the age of 12, I was already addicted to porn.

Until now, I had never shared that before.

I never thought about my purpose a lot but I had this inclination in me. I felt there was so much more to life than the environment that I was in and the things I was dealing with.

Now I know that was God.

He was giving me those little specks of hope. Even now, as I'm sitting here typing I can sense his hope, grace, and love. Being that I was a foster child and dealing with all these things, I didn't sense a piece of purpose. Actually, for a while I asked God why did I have to go through so much at a young age? The rejection I felt because of my mom or dad not being able to get us back was real. Some of you may have a similar past. You may have been abused physically, mentally, or even emotionally. God wants to use those things to do amazing things through you. I spent years searching for fulfilment in things, people, places, accomplishments. But nothing worked. Not only did I have to deal with my own demons, but there are also generational curses that run in my family. So, things that I had no power over were overtaking me as well. But that all changed when I found my purpose in life.

I remember it like it was literally yesterday. I had been saved for a couple of years already. I was at my second job. I was 21 years old. Every time I was at church, I begged God to reveal my purpose to me. When I spent time with Him I kept asking Him. I know God was like okay, okay daughter I get it. That day I was dealing with confusion, I just didn't know what I was doing in life. Well, for some reason, I began to search a topic on google. I came across this article and the article was basically a woman who mentored little girls. As I read her advice to them the Holy Spirit gently said, "Your purpose is to be an example of purity to young girls." Immediately I began to cry. I just knew that this was God because this overwhelming amount of peace was around me. Not only that, I knew His voice. Some may think I cried because of joy, no it was the complete opposite I cried because I couldn't believe that this was my purpose and this was how God was going to use me. This whole time, I begged and begged to know and then when He revealed it I immediately felt inadequate. I felt shame, because the life that I was living even on this day was not one of purity. I was still sleeping with my boyfriend, and doing other things that only God knew about. So of course, I felt that way. I was looking at myself and who I was in that moment and not who God was seeing me as in the future. You see, when we ask God to reveal our purpose to us we should be okay with what He says. ***We must be willing to go through the process to get there.*** Not only that, we must believe it! Shortly after Him revealing this to me, I ran in the complete opposite direction. I mean I ran so much I had dreams about running. The reason I was running is because I still felt like I wasn't good enough for this vision that God showed me, and I was afraid of failing. You see I only have three biological younger brothers, no sisters. But when I was adopted I immediately had four sisters, two younger and two older. God was preparing me in my own home to fulfill my purpose but I couldn't see. That's why Romans 8:28 is one of my favorite verses "And we know that ALL things work together for those who love the Lord and are called according to His purpose and plan." It gives those of us who have been through really hard times hope that it will all make sense in the end. You may be in a place where you don't know what is going on in your life. Well guess what, there is someone who knows every hair that is on your head. His name is Jesus and he has a plan for your life!

A specific purpose only YOU can fulfill! Yes You!

The awesome thing about God is He never holds your past against you; you can seek Him today and find out why you're here. So I told you that I ran from God when He told me why I was here. It didn't work. Because of where I was and my past, I began to think that was who I was. When God sees us, first he sees His son or daughter, if you are a child of God. Secondly He sees us as a finished product. How awesome is that! So forget what you are dealing with right now, it's not who you are! You are who He says you are! You are loved. You are special, peculiar, chosen, a royal priesthood, holy, and most of all you are His. So you may say okay I'm ready to play my Royal Position. I am ready to be the Queen that God has already called me to be! Well lets get into how to do that. I had to accept who God made me to be, and let me tell you it wasn't easy but it is so worth it. Once you accept who you are, you can allow God to help you discover why you are. So step one accept what God has said about you. For some of us, it will be hard, especially if you have attached who you are to the things you have experienced in your life. YOU are NOT what happened to you, or even what others have attached to you. So you have to take the word of God and only speak what he says you are.

The next thing is you must seek God.

I know this may sound cliché however it is not. If you want to know why you are here, you must seek the one who created you. Without the creator we won't know. We will spend years looking for something that was in us (through Him) the whole time. The bible says if you seek Him you will find Him. Seek Him with everything within you Queen. How do I do that? I'm glad you asked! So I would suggest first if you don't have one get a life application study bible in a version that you can understand thoroughly. Once you get this, I would suggest setting aside five, ten, or fifteen minutes; you decide how much time you have for Jesus. Does it take all of this Queen? YES! The more time you spend with God, the more you will be able to get familiar with his voice. The more you know His voice, the more He can direct your life. Also the more you know God the more you will become confident in who He has made you. Queen remember, when you know your purpose and who you are, it changes your whole life in such a beautiful and powerful way!! You will finally know why somethings happened the way they did! It will ALL lead back to your purpose and your calling! So this part is very critical! Start small and work your way up. What do you need to read? I got you sis! Start with who Jesus is, the Gospel's are a great place to start – Mark, Matthew, Luke, and John. The more you know Who God is, the more you will begin to trust that He knows what is best for you. He cares about everything concerning you; He can be trusted to guide you. Then look up scriptures about Him answering. He will answer. Be ready for when He reveals it to you. Most times He uses people, but make sure you feel peace about it.

So in the meantime while you waiting for God to direct you specifically, don't just sit still. Waiting doesn't mean that you are to be immobile. While I waited on God to reveal his way to me, I served. A lot of people forget this. Serve whether it be in your community, church, or with a non-profit. Something that you are passionate about is a perfect place to start. I think that we sometimes think too much. God gave you a personality, are you an introvert, extrovert, or semi? Do you enjoy big crowds? Are you more of an outside person? Or do you thrive in small intimate settings? SERVE!! While I was waiting on God I served everywhere! I was on choir, dance, I taught, I signed up for every fundraiser, and even things outside of church. I volunteered at non-profits, through different community programs.

When you are moving and serving you are more likely to bump into your lane.

This also shows God that you are committed to waiting and working. As I served in these different places, it ended up leading me closer to where God wanted me to be. SO SERVE!! Give back to someone else. I know a lot of women who are just sitting still and doing nothing and expecting God to just magically show them why they are here. Don't be that woman! There are gifts in you that others need! Use them by serving!!!

The final Step Ladies!!! Just a disclaimer that this is not a definite way of doing things. You may do some things differently. I am just giving some advice based on my experience. With that being said, submit is the final step. You should have known! So of course once God reveals your purpose or leads you to it you have to walk it out. I know that this has been the hardest part for me. I did run in the beginning. But I realized that God created me to be all that He has made me. Not only that, but there are people in the world that are waiting on me to walk in my calling. I believe sometimes we allow our own fears and anxieties to hold us back; but just think about your future and how it will look without your submission. So many people live their whole lives below who God made them to be. Listen Queen you will not be "those people". You will submit yourself to the call God has on your life. Even if you have to do it day by day. Whatever it takes! Remember that knowing and walking in your purpose will affect every aspect of your life. There is a fulfillment that comes from knowing why you're here! I can't even begin to tell you how amazing it has been to know my lane and to be okay and confident in where I fit in. However, not walking in your calling also will affect your life. You will never be satisfied, and it's also a form of settling. Walking in my purpose has brought me so much direction and guidance in my life. I have accepted or declined job opportunities based on my purpose. I have chosen who to date and not to date because of my purpose. I have chosen where to live, who to keep in my life and who to let go based on it. Knowing that I am a teacher has been the best thing outside of salvation to happen to me. Submitting to the creator of the universe will forever change and better your life. I don't know where you are right now, but if you woke up this morning with breath in your body **YOU CAN START!**

The main thing that held me back from submitting sooner wasn't other people or my past it was ME. I couldn't see past myself and how afraid I was. But the more I spent time with my Father, He told me it's not only about you! Submitting to your purpose Queen can change generations after you. Your children and your children's children. Not only your bloodline but what about the billions of other people in this world who are waiting on you. One day we will all stand before God and I don't know about you, but I want to hear "Well done my good and faithful servant"

Q.U.E.E.N Tip

So, you may be saying okay I'm READY! Queen, take one day at a time. This walking in purpose is a journey, not a destination. Take your time, heal from the inside out, and grow. Submit to your purpose, it will all be worth it in the end.

About the Author

Terquieshin (Tee) Pringle born in South Carolina is a young profound teacher and leader of this generation. Not coming from the best of situations, she gave her life to God at the tender age of 15. Although saved; she didn't realize the level of awareness, influence and favor that God had bestowed upon her life until she was 21. At that age she embraced the call of God over her life to unapologetically teach, motivate and inspire the younger generation.

Tee has 3 biological siblings and 7 adopted siblings.

Currently a teacher/volunteer in the R.E.A.L program with Daybreak Ministries which focuses on teaching/training young girls on how to build healthy relationships, empowering them to make wise decisions, and teaching them how to build their relationship with Christ.

Tee also is a Youth Leader at Truth Church and Ministries under the covering of Pastor Andrew Jones. In addition to teaching, Tee is currently finishing her undergrad degree in Psychology. Upon completion she desires to become a therapist for children in Foster Care system.

She believes that with God, NOTHING IS IMPOSSIBLE!

Connect with this Queen via

IG: iamhis1107

FB: Tee Pringle

* * * * * * * * * * * * * * * * * *

God's Extravagance, Presence, and Favor

By: Colleen Batchelder

"Because of the extravagance of those revelations, and so I wouldn't get a big head, I was given the gift of a handicap to keep me in constant touch with my limitations…" – 2 Corinthians 12:7 MSG

ecause of the extravagance, I keep rereading this verse and thinking about the beauty, and majesty, and perfection of God. If we look back in scripture, we'll find countless moments of men and women standing in awe of the greatness of God. We'll also find countless moments of men and women standing still because they feared the greatness of God.

Sometimes, our greatest deterrent is not the potential of failure, but the potential of success. It is the realization that we have the breath of God in our lungs, the purpose of Christ in our steps, and a powerful call on our life. This compels us to move. However, success is never met with ease.

In 2 Corinthians 5:14, the Apostle Paul calls us to be constrained or compelled by the love of Christ. However, when we take that first step, we are convinced by the extravagance. This starts us in the right direction. It gives us the ability to leap with both feet into the venture that God has for us. However, in order to finish the race, we must be convinced of the presence of God to labor for the purpose of God.

When I first started LOUD Summit, my mind whirled. I was compelled and commissioned with such purpose. I didn't want to wait another minute before enacting this plan and setting this prayer in motion. I was convinced by the extravagance; however, after three years of sweat, and rejection, and frustration, and setbacks, I quickly lost my energy and needed something more sustaining. This is when I became convinced of the presence of God and the favor of God.

When you understand that God is with you and that God is for you, it's easy to find rest, peace, and strength to accomplish your dreams.

However, if you're waiting for your emotions to validate your calling, you'll be swayed by the haters, deterred by the hard work, and depleted by the long journey.

When the emotions fade and you feel like giving up, your faith has to grow deeper, and your resolution has to grow stronger. You need to be convinced of the extravagance of God, the presence of God, and the favor of God.

Q. uit Making Excuses

- Learn to rest in the presence of God
- Go deeper in your faith when God seems quiet
- Don't quit in the moment when your journey gets tough
- Think about how your calling empowers those around you
- Surround yourself with other Q.U.E.E.N.S. who are living out their calling

U. nderstand Your Assignment

> I have been called for this time, for this moment, and for this generation.

There is power in our presence when we acknowledge the presence of God. We serve a God who has a passion and heart to love people. LOUD Summit was born out of a desire to see young people empowered, encouraged, and equipped to live out their destiny. This is why I created a space where the skeptic could seek answers, feel welcomed, and be fully loved. God has used LOUD to start the conversation. We've created and presented workshops on purpose, mental health, racial reconciliation, and human trafficking within the confines of New York City and are preparing to launch our second summit in 2020 in Jacksonville, FL.

> God has called us to expand and impact young people throughout the country and around the world.

However, my greatest prayer for LOUD, is that we would remain a City on a Hill and a safe haven of inclusion and community. My greatest prayer is that LOUD would be a movement that would encourage, empower, and equip leaders to have a love for people and a love for Christ.

E. nlist Your Supporting Cast

My team has been an incredible beacon of prayer, support, accountability, and leadership. They are the partners of this incredible movement of God, and I thank God daily for them. They are the people that paint the canvas of LOUD Summit and fellow leaders who help to cast the vision.

E. stablish Your Winning Team

Encourage dissension. If you choose people who look like you, act like you, vote like you, and think like you, then you will create an organization in your image, and not for the benefit of others. The greatest piece of advice I could give you, would be to embrace and encourage diversity. This need to be purposeful on the part of the CEO. Make sure that your board is diversified in gender, race, denomination, political view, and perspective. This ensures that your vision is influential and not insular.

N. ow

> Every day is my NOW moment.

You don't just wake up and decide that today is the day that you will stop making excuses, you must choose to change your perspective and choose your NOW each morning. When you step out in your calling, you'll be faced with lots of NOW moments. As a Christian single female CEO and minister, it's never been easy to live out my God-given calling within the church.

> ## I have had doors shut in my face due to my singleness, my gender, my purpose, and my education.

Education in many circles is celebrated; however, in others, it's seen as a lack of faith, a stance of doubt, and a quest of pride. I've always been intellectual. I'm the nerd who used to translate Shakespeare for fun and delve into theology books for light reading. However, leadership and academia are not always encouraged, especially amongst women within the church. For some reason, some leaders see educated women as a threat, instead of a blessing. Similarly, many churches still do not provide women the opportunity to utilize their pastoral gifts fully.

Being a single woman in fulltime ministry has been interesting. There's always the underlying assumption that I'm unfulfilled or lacking in some way because of my gender and my relationship status. However, that couldn't be further from the truth. I love being single. I love the freedom that I have to travel and speak all over. I love that I can further my education or take up a new hobby. Most of all, I love that it gives me the chance to help my parents and be there for them as they get older.

There are many moments of NOW that we have to face. Some bigger than others. However, when we understand WHO we are, it's easier to live out WHAT we're called to do.

Q.U.E.E.N Tip

Understand who you are and press into the extravagance, presence, and favor of God. The road won't be easy, but the view at the top will be worth the journey.

Q.U.E.E.N Prayer

Dear Lord God,

Thank you that you have awesome plans for these readers. I pray that you would give them clarity, boldness, bravery, and stamina to keep going when they feel like giving up. Give them a glimpse of your extravagance, a glimpse of your presence, and glimpse of your favor. Give them the fullness of who you are so that they can step into the fullness of their calling!

In Jesus' Name,

Amen

About the author

Colleen Batchelder is the Founder and President of LOUD Summit – an organization for those in their 20s and 30s that presents workshops, seminars, and summits that encourage, empower and equip this generation to live out their destiny and walk in their purpose.

She speaks at conferences, churches, companies, and colleges on intergenerational communication, marketing, branding your vision and living authentically in a 'filtered' world.

In addition, she consults with companies and aid organizations in their quest to create teams that function from a place of intergenerational communication that bridges the generational gap.

When not studying for her DMin in Leadership and Global Perspectives at Portland Seminary, you can find her enjoying a nice Chai Latte, exploring NYC, or traveling to a new and exotic destination.

Let's Get Social Queen

www.LOUDSummit.com | www.colleenbatchelder.org | IG: @loud_summit

* * * * * * * * * * * * * * * * * * *

Bloom where you're planted

By: Robyn Mobley

For the Spirit God gave us does not make us timid, but gives us power, love and self-discipline. 2 Timothy 1:7 KJV

Everything I asked God for, he's blessed me with.

I never had a plan for the way I envisioned my life. I'm a "go with the flow" kind of person. However, I believe that stems from a fear of rejection or not being "good enough." I'm not the best Christian. I don't go to church every Sunday, or bible study on Wednesdays. However, I trust and know God. I pray more than anything and I know where all my blessings come from. God is the head of everything I do and have. With experience, I know my faith will grow stronger and my discipline in His word will become a lifestyle.

Q. uit Making Excuses

I always share my college experience because this is when my faith for God was solidified. While in school, I "skated" through. I did the bear minimum to get by and boy did it show. By my junior year, my guidance counselor informed me that I would not be able to start my field placement due to my GPA. Without this internship, I could not graduate on time with my BSW. I had to decide. Did I want to graduate with a sociology degree in which I had no interest in or did I want to stay another year in school and pick up a minor? As a young adult, who feared making those tough decisions, I leaned on God. If I knew nothing else, I knew he wouldn't have brought me this far to leave me. I decided to stay another year and take responsibility for my actions. God blew my mind that "bonus" year of college. For trusting him and my journey, he blessed me with a competitive internship that I thought I wasn't interested in. He also blessed me to receive a stipend with the promise of obtaining employment within the social work field after I graduated. In this moment, I saw God's word manifest in my life.

U. nderstand Your Assignment

I am a child welfare social worker. My role is to ensure the safety of children and assist with reunifying a parent with their children. I wear many hats in this role as one could imagine. At the point a child is in foster care, their parent isn't always "ready" to do the work to reunify with their child or children. So, I am their "guardian." I assist the foster parent or kinship placement with meeting the child's daily needs. I also work with their parents to meet the needs identified at the time of removal. God uses me daily to be the support the family needs day in and day out. I'm asked often how I do the job that I do. I always say, "it is my calling by God." Every day I wake up and don't know what to expect. I don't know what role I will play, what's coming my way or how the day will be. However, I know that I trust God and I'm exactly where I need to be. I believe my assignment is to help people. The faith that they lack, I have and I'm able to use it to uplift them. I can share my testimony to encourage them on days that don't seem clear. The rapport that I have with anyone I meet allows my families to trust me as in reality, I hold their lives in my hand as their social worker. I do not believe this is my only assignment however, I'm exactly where I need to be at this moment.

E. nlist Your Supporting Case

Naturally, my support came from my mother; now husband; family and friends. The supportive people I have in my life, never gave me the opportunity to ask for help. They automatically support me in any and everything thing I do and vice versa. My village believes in me more than I believe in myself. They know what I need when I need it. My mother often reminds me to trust God when I start to question my purpose or want to give up. My husband reminds me of my worth and the joy I bring to others effortlessly. My friends are all successful public service workers which consist of teachers, nurses, human resource workers and social workers. They share a lot of my challenges. Their success pushes me past my goals. I'm surrounded by success which encourages me to be more.

E.stablish Your Winning Team

> I didn't assign anyone to be a supportive person in my life. God aligned those in my life to be here for a season or for a lifetime.

There are friends that I've had for years who supported me throughout a season. We may no longer speak however, they fulfilled their purpose in my journey and for that, I'm grateful. I'm selective with whom I choose to associate myself with, so I haven't had a negative impact of my support system. When deciding who will be a support in your life, choose those who are growing with you or who are successful before you. They can serve as a positive support and can guide you along the way. Your whole team should be winning, and they should be helping you get where they are.

N. ow

I am a woman living the "American dream." I'm happily married with our first child, Olivia Mobley. I'm growing within my career. We're home owners and are stable. I say all this not to brag or boast. However, I decided to truly break from fear, uncertainty or doubt when God provided us with all he knew our hearts desired. Often, I say, "God continues to bless us even when we're not deserving." God gets all the glory and honor for or many blessings. I decided to make the decision to simply live. Go after the things I want and trust that if it's in Gods will for me and my family, it'll be ours. I now understand, rejection or denial is not always a negative thing. God is simply telling me several things. I'm not ready, it's not what he has planned for me or he's shielding me from something to protect me. Everything that glitters ain't gold. I no longer allow the negative to control my future. This can pertain to family, career, spiritual, etc. I have a lot of growing and learning to do. I'm young and inexperienced in so many things. However, by the grace of God, I'm here. I'm learning and willing to do what's needed to soar. For now, I'll continue to learn, grow and lean on the Lord to trust my journey.

Q.U.E.E.N Tip

DO YOU! Don't focus on what other people are doing.

Focus on what you want and your purpose. If someone is doing something and you genuinely want to do it, do it. Trust yourself and trust that God will lead you in your divine purpose and you will SOAR.

"To give anything less than your best is to sacrifice a gift."

Q.U.E.E.N PRAYER

Lord, I thank you for the opportunity to share our journey. I thank you for being the light. I pray for each reader, participate, author and co-author. I pray for whoever reads our journey that we're able to answer any questions they may have for their current situation. I pray that they would lean on your word and trust you as you will provide all that their hearts desire according to your perfect Will. I pray for peace, growth, freedom and prosperity.

In Jesus name, Amen.

About the Author

Robyn Mobley is a 27-year-old millennial Queen, originally from Bridgeport, Connecticut. At the age of seven, her family moved to Charlotte, NC where she was raised by a single mother. She is the middle child of three and holds a bachelor's in social work from North Carolina Agricultural and Technical State University. She currently has a thriving career in social work at the Union County Department of Social Services and resides with her beloved husband and beautiful one year old daughter.

Connect with this Queen:

Facebook: Robyn K Mobley   Instagram: @_mrs.mobley

Email: robyn.harris26@yahoo.com

* * * * * * * * * * * * * * * * * * *

Who God Calls You to Be

By: Aya Mhlongo

"Finally, my brethren, be strong in the Lord, and in the power of his might." Ephesians 6:10 KJV

Sometimes, I wish I could turn back time. Go back to my childhood, a simpler time.

Correct all my mistakes.

Being a 24-year-old mom to a 3-year-old has not been a walk in the park.

And having no parents or even supportive relatives does help either.

I've always been creative with an entrepreneurial spirit. I have been in love with anything that has to do with fashion since 7th grade. I remember overhearing a former classmate mentioning a career path in fashion design. Since then, I just knew that I had to pursue that field. So with little to no funds for formal get education in my childhood dream field, YouTube became my best friend. I remember my mother purchasing my first sewing machine. I instantly came up with gazillions of cool business ideas *that all failed*.

#Facts- some didn't even get off the ground because at that time I lacked patience and consistency.

Shortly after losing my mother, I had my daughter. My child's father was present; but the thought of depending on a man worried me.

My mother was the bravest woman I knew in our community. She had no husband; through hard work and prayer she built a home for her three daughters; took all three of us to school and raised us to be strong fearless independent women.

Now I have a human being who I'm totally responsible for plus my own dreams of owning a successful company and a beautiful home. Those thoughts made me think that maybe all I need is a stable salary, so job hunting was my next plan. At least I knew for sure that with a stable income, myself and my baby would be taken care of.

So I got my first job EVER at a call center company. I worked as a Quality assurance agent (listening to recorded phone calls between clients and agents). I met lovely people there, I even started selling weaves and bags to gain an extra income, **but the working hours were horrible.**

I hardly spent time with my baby, had little to no 'me time', and the salary was worse. I left that job without a plan because my body couldn't take it anymore.

I clocked out from a night shift one morning and sent my supervisor a

> "I'm not coming back, I found a new job" WhatsApp text.

The following day I tried to convince myself to just stick to having my own business because the corporate world isn't a nice place; *it's only good when it's pay day.*

> Two days later it's back to dreading the week, I couldn't live like that anymore.

I then came up with a gift box business idea~ it was great. I loved it and saw a lot of sales potential, but it wasn't big on profit unless I charged ridiculous prices. Unfortunately for me, I don't believe in over charging people for doing what I *love*.

> Then the devil called self-doubt came in and convinced me to just go back to the corporate world.

So, I went out and got a second (*last*) job; I fought and prayed so hard to get that job. It was a bigger and better call center company this time; still doing the same work as my previous job. I was over joyed because this meant I would finally get my own little first apartment and hopefully a car before the year ended. Because I'm not a morning person and dislike travelling through morning and afternoon traffic, I then decided to move closer to work.

I moved in on a Sunday and on Monday I got dismissed from work.

At first, I felt let down by God.

I had everything that I had prayed for and lost it all the next day.

But there was a voice at a back of my mind; it kept reminding me that God does not burden a soul beyond what it can bear. "Cast all your anxiety on Him because He cares for you. - 1 Peter 5:7". I put my faith in him and I knew that he would come through for me.

I didn't know how or when that would be; however;

I had no worries because I praise a living God.

This entire situation helped me to realize that the standard nine to five life was not for me.

Unfortunately, most of my friends and family don't believe in entrepreneurship~ especially start-ups.

They would support my job-hunting decisions but not my business ideas.

I thank God that I don't need anyone's validation to succeed and I really appreciate those who have been there when I needed someone to talk to, to cheer me up, encourage and support my dreams.

I'm currently working on my bag making business again. I love it like I did when I first started years ago. I'm taking things slowly, I'm continuing to learn on YouTube, I follow people who do the same thing as me, and I'm inspired and motivated. **I have big plans.**

I'm excited; the possibilities of what awaits me excite me beyond words.

Q.U.E.E.N Tip

'If the plan fails, change the plan but never the goal.'

I am my only limit.

A very cute bonus to this situation is that I get to spend more time with my baby, work at my own time and space, and **no more early morning alarms.**

I might not be getting a car before the year ends or the vacations I hoped for soon, but I thank God for everything. I genuinely want to work on my business. I want to make it a success. *I believe I can!*

I know I'll have doubts and feel unmotivated some days,

but prayer is my buddy.

Whatever achievements, whatever worries I share with my God, my friends and my very own handpicked family I will always rise again and again because with every storm comes sunshine.

Q.U.E.E.N TIP

Follow your heart and never ever settle!!! Remember ~ a smooth sea never made a skilled sailor, do not be afraid of failure, Because failure is only the opportunity to begin again, only this time more wisely. Believe in yourself Queen!

About the Author

Ayanda "Aya" Mhlongo, a 24-year-old handbag designer and entrepreneur and mommy to a very busy toddler. born and bred in Johannesburg, South Africa, her handbag brand is called Aya M.

Connect with our Queen

Facebook Aya Mhlongo

Twitter @ayamhlongo1

Instagram as @ayamhlongo

Email address is mhlongoaya94@gmail.com.

* * * * * * * * * * * * * * * * * * * *

Prosper in the Lord

By: Jessica Merino

"For I know the plans I have for you declares the Lord, plans to prosper you and not to harm. You, plans to give you hope and a future." Jeremiah 29:11

hroughout life, we face many hurdles and barriers that put a hindrance on our growth and development. For me, it was believing in myself. For many years self-belief was my biggest struggle, so I looked for validation from the outside world which led me directly into a toxic relationship.

When I found a man that comforted me, consoled me, and confirmed my identity it made me feel special.

I became hooked to the false love interpreted as real love in my spiritual darkness.

Living in a carnal world, I had carnal thoughts. I was unable to spiritually discern the obvious presence of the enemy in my life.

I was blinded by my physical, material and sexual lust.

I morphed into a woman who eventually lost her identity.

This led to my downfall, my rock bottom, my story.

I always knew that I had a higher power within. I knew that the current state of being was not my destiny or God's plan for me. I didn't know how to bring out the influential, herculean, high powered and compelling woman I knew I was supposed to be. I can remember clearly the dissatisfaction in my life and how broken I felt with such little faith, strength, or desire.

Seeing other women experience similar feelings, or choices that I made would unsettle me. "All they have to do is break away" I would say; but who was I to help them magnify their spirit or enlighten their direction when I was in the same circumstance?

I knew that whatever I chose to do in life, it had to impact women from all over the world. Women who were disinclined to take that first step forward because of their crippling unbelief. It was essential that I become the very woman I needed for counseling and direction. I aspired to be the woman that I needed when I was in displeasure. Becoming a servant of Christ allows me to uplift, teach, and create effective avenues for women who are fearful of the unknown, with little to no belief at all.

> Knowing that there are women connected to me through affliction, is why I serve to impact her, you, and us.

Visions of becoming a business owner would haunt me. I worked for companies throughout life that never felt settling. The feeling of being caged in, allowing someone to tell me how much money I was worth or when I deserved a raise was *dispiriting*. I believed I had immense value so I would naturally draw my attention towards successful people that I looked up to, whether it was watching an inspirational video or reading a book about faith. I immersed myself into successful peoples' lives so much that I started to think, and talk like them. I was determined to start my business by any means. I started to follow successful people on social media so much that most of my timeline was filled with positivity.

I remember coming across a lovely woman who would post about starting your own traveling business daily. She was literally in my face with this perfect opportunity, but I was so hesitant to start because once again my unbelief would creep up. **With the power of prayer and faith,** I started my own home-based traveling agency business. That leap of small leap of faith has since taken off. My entire atmosphere and *flavor* of life have changed.

I noticed that I began to attract different people towards me by projecting pure, positive and supportive energy. God was placing the right people at the right time in my life.

He was creating my success team while I was coming into alignment spiritually.

I was able to discern the right people clearly by the way we all connected through prayer, the same obstacles we faced. Our drives were explosive, and we constantly supported each other.

It was important for me to keep a positive atmosphere and not allow myself to look back at the old me. The more I kept positive people around me the more drive I had, the more spirit and the urge to keep going. They wouldn't let me fail or neglect my dreams which in turn trained me to treat myself as such. I was more attentive to the things and people surrounding me to keep going in the direction I had to go.

Failure was no longer allowed in my space.

The building up to this point in life surely did not come easy or unchallenging. As I mentioned in the beginning, I hit rock bottom.

I had to be afflicted to find my way and hear God clearly.

Real Talk

I didn't understand this process at the time.

I had to walk away from a toxic relationship that I had depended on financially, mentally and emotionally for such a long time. It was unpleasant and unwelcoming to say the least.

I remember living- roaming from hotel to hotel, sleeping on someone else's living room floor, and sometimes- sleeping in my car in the middle of winter~ using the car heater just to stay warm.

As a single mother, not knowing what you're going to feed your kids on any given day is heartbreaking and upsetting.

I lost all hope and felt like a failure to my children and to myself.

I remember working third shift at the very hotel I lived in for very little money and just enough to get by while working my business. *I wasn't going to give up that easy.*

Then there were shameful times, where my children's friends would want to come over and play with my kids after school. Nobody knew that we lived in a hotel, so we'd always use the excuse that we were leaving out of town for a trip.

I remember having every opportunity and door slammed in my face.

I experienced every no, every brick wall, and every barrier to the point where it felt like I was dying.

It felt as if I were a prisoner of my own life.

> I couldn't set myself free or catch a break. How did I get here?

I remember asking myself. How did I fall this hard?

I remember looking at my kids and telling them "just hold on a little while longer ~ it'll all be over soon." I was always frantic and worried about where the kids and I would sleep or eat that day. The enemy wouldn't allow me to hear God clearly so, time and time again I would try to handle it my way.

Funny thing is, that it doesn't work that way, life just doesn't work without God.

I had to fall to the lowest place to hear God clearly and to feel his presence. I had to get to the point in life where I had no other option but to *fall to my knees and surrender.*

When I opened my heart and eyes to God, I heard my calling clearly.

Supernatural things began to happen in my life. The only resources I had were Gods word and prayer. It was then that I began to feel the Holy Spirit move in my life.

It was the most beautiful, divine feeling ever.

The closer I got to God, the more I could feel his breath pressed upon my cheeks as a reminder that He will never leave me or forsake me. That he was always there and to never be afraid.

Doors would open unexpectedly.

Opportunities were coming left, right and from above.

I was excited about the new endeavors that were opening for me.

For the first time, my path was uncomplicated and translucent.

I know that I will still face challenges throughout life.

It'll just be different this time because no weapon formed against me will ever prosper.

Q.U.E.E.N Tip

Remember to never cancel your appointment in Gods appointment book. You are not Rejected. No matter how much chaos is going on around you ~ He sees you. The blueprint of your life was never lost in the crowd. Queen, He knows your heart and your mind.

And when you open the eyes of your heart, He'll speak to you. I know what it feels like when difficulties arise, just remember…

He still chose you.

We serve a God who meets our every need.

All the tears and pain never go unnoticed. Seek him. Follow him.

There is a blessing at the end of your battle.

"I pray that out of his glorious riches he may strengthen you with power, through his spirit in your inner being." Ephesians 3:16

About the Author

Jessica Merino resides in Kalamazoo Michigan. She is the CEO & owner of Unforgettable Escapes Traveling Agency. She has an insatiable passion for motivating, inspiring and helping people become the BEST version of themselves. She hopes to help others cross over from struggle to Victory in Jesus Christ. In her spare time, she enjoys reading, traveling, exercising, and socializing.

Connect with this Queen

Email: unfortableescapes1@gmail.com

Facebook: Jessi Merino

Facebook group: Unforgettable Escapes Traveling Agency

Instagram: jmer7

* * * * * * * * * * * * * * * * * * *

God's Plan

By: Ylonda Powell

"For I know the plans I have for you," declares the Lord, "Plans to prosper you and not to harm you, plans to give you hope and a future." Jeremiah 9:11 NIV

*L**ife brings many ups and downs* and we must always remember that God has predestined our lives for such a time as this. He has given us gifts, talents, dreams and ideas to edify the Kingdom. As we stay in His will and use our gifts to the glory of God we will reap the benefits with ***great expectation*** and a remarkable future. Ephesians 2:10 reads "For we are God's handiwork, created in Christ Jesus to do good works, which God prepared in advance for us to do." God has made us all with gifts and talents and

He expects us to use them while we are here on earth.

Ponder this~ if you gave someone a gift and you knew that that gift will enrich their lives. You purchased it just for them to use.

What if they opened it and never used it or worst ~opened it and just put it on a shelf?

Most people would take great offense to that.

Now imagine all the people in this world that have never used their God given talents.

I would like to share some of the highs and lows about my journey of pursuing my dreams as an actress, writer, producer and director. Make no mistakes about it~ my good days outweigh my bad days.

Growing up, I lived in a single-family home. I lived with my mother and had a relationship with my father outside the home. I never felt unloved by either of my parents even though there was friction at times. I grew up in the inner city of New Haven, CT and attended public schools. My mother made sure that I attended church regularly, but most importantly she instilled a real relationship with Jesus Christ.

At a early age, I knew what my talents and passions consisted of. I remember as a young girl, I would dress up in my mother's clothes and high heels and put a towel on my head. I had to make sure I placed one of those plastic head bands, so the towel wouldn't fall off as I ran around the house *pretending to be a movie star*. A family friend and I would often write skits and perform them at family gatherings and church. I remember my mother taking me to go see the movie Annie when I was eight years old. I was so captivated by the little girl on the screen.

I recall uttering the words *"I can do that"* while watching the movie. I knew at that very moment, that I wanted to be an actress. For middle school, I attended Betsy Ross Arts Magnet School. My favorite artistic subjects were theater and dance. Little did I know that being enrolled at Betsy Ross would present an opportunity of a lifetime and start my professional career as an actress.

One day in 1987 while sitting in class in sixth grade, there was an announcement over the PA system. The announcement was about auditions for a stage play at Yale Repertory Theater. I remember being so excited. I went home and told my mother that I wanted to audition. The audition was scheduled, and the day had come. I recall being excited, yet nervous at the same time.

I was called into the room and read the lines and then was asked to sing. Singing was not and still isn't my thing. So my answer was "No". Unbeknownst to me, I had just refused to sing to two theater legends the late playwright August Wilson and the late legendary director Lloyd Richards. **Back then I didn't know what favor from God was, BUT His favor was obviously on my life.**

I booked the role of Maretha in the groundbreaking stage play Piano Lessons starring a rising and now superstar Samuel L. Jackson, Rocky Carroll, the late Carl Gordon, Starletta Dubious and others. I made history with being one of the original cast members of Piano Lessons. God was paving the way and preparing me at a young age for great destiny. I must add that my mom told me if I wanted to stay in the play I had to keep my grades up.

Momma didn't play that!

Needless to say, that was the first time I ever received honors. We still laugh about that. I still remember that experience and will cherish it for the rest of my life.

As time went on I continued to audition for community and church plays. I was landing almost every leading role that I auditioned for. My confidence in my acting ability was high and I knew that I had a bright future in "Hollywood". **Those were my plans, but it took some time to realize God had another path for my life.**

The year was 1994 ~ I was eighteen years old. Fresh out of high school and off to college to fulfill my "parents dreams" of furthering my education. My grades were okay in the beginning, but then they began to slip as time went on. My heart, mind and soul wanted to pursue a career in acting. **In 1997, I decided to leave college and pursue my dream.**

Earlier I mentioned that I was taught to build a relationship with Christ and to pray that His will be done in my life. I always had a great love for Christ and wanted to please Him in every area of my life.

I soon learned that my will and the Lord's will did not mix. It was either my way or His way. When you are set apart from the beginning of time God will frustrate your plans, so His divine will can be done.

"Father, if you are willing, please take this cup of suffering away from me. Yet I want your will to be done, not mine." Luke 22;42.

Little did I know that the price of being set apart and anointed would shake me to the core at times. As a young adult, I began to take my relationship with Christ seriously and knew that He had His hand me. However, I wanted to make it in Hollywood as a big film and television actress. There was a time when I was a teenager that my mom told me that I would one day produce and direct productions. I wasn't feeling that at all. I was destined to be an actress and an actress only, so I thought. ***I only wanted to be in front of the camera or in the spotlight not behind it.***

I became a member of Prayer Tabernacle Church of Love. Here is where God began to reveal other gifts, talents and fulfill what my mother had prophesied to me. I was asked to write a skit for a woman's program. I remember saying to myself "I don't write", but I went home and came up with a five page skit. I gathered some actors and performed the skit. The congregation loved it. I said to myself "well that's over". A few weeks later my Pastor asked me to write a play for the Christmas program. Again, I said "I am not a writer", but out of obedience I wrote a twenty page play. The congregation loved it. ***At that moment I began to feel that I was on to something.*** I began to write, produce and direct skits and plays at the church for special occasions.

Also, during this time, I began to take my acting career to the next level. I took professional head shots and starting traveling to The Big Apple (NYC). As I began to pursue my career in NYC, I quickly realized that it was a totally different ball game than back home. The competition was much greater, the pool of talent there was just as serious as I was, and they wanted that big break just as bad as I did. I began to submit my head shot and resume to various auditions and started getting callbacks. I would travel from New Haven to NYC a few times a week for casting calls. I felt that my dreams were finally coming true!

As much as I was pursuing my career I was putting that same energy in my walk with Christ. I felt like I was thriving in both areas until I started to feel uneasy about the direction my acting career was going. The casting agents were calling me in for parts that did not agree with my spirit. *I was getting calls for roles full of profanity and even nudity.*

I began to turn down roles because I just couldn't bring myself to perform in that manner. *I remember being told by a couple of people in the industry "do you know what you are turning down" and "you have to be an actress first and then you can be a Christian later".*

For the first time I was at a crossroad between my faith and my career.

I felt that God was redirecting my life and career in a different direction.

Still wanting this so badly, I moved to White Plains, NY at one point and then the Bronx so I could be closer and more readily available to audition. A few months later I had to move back home both times because things just weren't going as planned. A few months later I went to Los Angeles with hopes of pursuing a career in film and television, but a week later had to move back to Connecticut because the plans I HAD MADE fell through.

When I arrived back to Connecticut I was depressed. I felt like a failure and didn't know what to do at that point. I was in a dark place because I didn't understand why God allowed these doors to be closed. I remember a time when I persistently pursued meeting someone in the industry that could potentially "put me on". He finally called me for an audition and month later died in a car accident. I was devastated and questioned God about all the disappointments and heartache in pursuing something that I felt He wanted me to do.

God is so good that He will keep filling you with hope to get to the next level. After I began to pick myself up again *I felt God tugging on my heart to begin my own production company.* I didn't know the first thing about running a production company, *but I had big faith and a big God to back me.*

In 2001 Jesonda Productions was birthed.

In 2006, I started a performing arts school for children and teenagers. It was a thriving school for a number of years and had two locations. I began to feel alive again even though I had turned my focus a bit from acting to teaching. Owning my own production was not easy. Over the years I had opened several studios and had to close them over the years. That could be devastating to see the vision that you want and constantly have doors shut.

However, **I kept pursuing because when God has a plan for your life He will make sure to keep pushing you.**

In 2010, God had given me a groundbreaking storyline for some things I was experiencing in my life and saw from those around me.

I wrote the now hit stage play **Stuck**.

Embarking on this journey, I didn't realize, just how bittersweet it would be.

I knew that the Lord had His hand on this project and needed this message to be out. I remember hearing a voice inside my head saying, "it's time to get this message out". Being obedient to the voice, I began to maximize my resources and call family and friends who had theatrical experience. We began to rehearse with a half of script.

The week of the performance, I succinctly remember the Lord giving me the exact ending to my play. I rallied all my cast members and told them exactly what to say and where to move. Till this day, that portion of the play continues to be the most awe-inspiring and powerful part of the play.

After Stuck debuted with such great success and with standing room only, friction quickly started to take place in my life. Longtime relationships began to fall apart too. I was devastated and in deep pain over this. It took a while for me to understand that this scripture was what I needed to grasp and remember "For we wrestle not against flesh and blood, but against principalities, against powers, against the rulers of the darkness of this world, against spiritual wickedness in high places." Ephesians 6:12. I began to pray for strength to carry out this assignment and to learn to fight through any opposition through the Spirit.

I can almost guarantee that any dream chaser, especially one that has committed their gifts, talents and life to Jesus Christ has been through many ups, downs, misunderstandings, heartache, disappointments and sleepiness nights; but in the end, God shows Himself mighty. In the End, that is the Only thing that matters.

Q.U.E.E.N Tip

I had to learn that when you are on the right path that God has designed for you, trials and tribulations will come; but His promises are yes and amen. Keep dreaming, keep pursuing, keep praying, keep going you will reap if you faint not. Pursuing a dream and working towards goals in life can be bittersweet; but is it certainly worth it when He says, "Well done my good and faithful servant". Go get what God has for you!

About the Author:

Ylonda Powell is the CEO and Founder of Jesonda (Jesus and Ylonda) Productions- a renowned production company showcasing talented local artists in all things theatrical and more. She's been seen on "The Amen Corner," multiple media sources, and produced the stage hit play "Stuck." She resides with her loving husband and beautiful children.

Connect with this Queen

Fb @Ylonda Powell

IG @Ylondapm

website www.jesondaproductions.com

* * * * * * * * * * * * * * * * * * * *

Afterword

𝒯wo words

"My God!"

Queen, you were just given the blueprint to move from good to GREATER in Jesus Christ!

These dynamic leaders just left their heart, their wisdom, and love for HIM on the pages of this book.

Now Queen, it is left completely up to you.

You must choose.

Will you live for HIM and SOAR?

Or

Will you selfishly live for self and remain stagnant and stuck?

Remember Queen, You were designed for MORE, to do MORE and To Be More in the Body of Christ.

Don't delay on the Calling placed over your life.

Don't delay on taking the first steps- the Victory has already been won for you.

I want you to DREAM BIG, DREAM BOLD, and LIVE OUT YOUR GOD SIZED DREAMS!

YOU WERE CREATED FOR A TIME SUCH AS THIS!

QUEEN, IT'S TIME TO PLAY YOUR ROYAL POSITION

Queen, WILL YOU COME?

Maybe you read this entire book and still walked away feeling defeated?

Maybe you read this book and said "well, that was great for them, but I don't see my out- how can I play my royal position when I have lived a life of shame, hurt, and guilt?"

I want to invite you to have a Real relationship with Jesus.

I know Him to be a 'Way maker."

If you do not know Jesus Christ as your personal Lord and Savior, Queen I welcome you to know Him with this simple salvation prayer- Read Aloud:

Heavenly Father,

I am a sinner, in need of a Savior. Forgive me of my sins

Jesus Christ, I welcome you into my life on this day.

I recognize that I cannot Play my Royal Position on my own. I need you.

I believe that you are the son of God and died for my sins on Calvary.

You rose on the 3rd day so that I may be free in You.

I welcome you on this day. I worship you on this day and will serve you for the rest of my life.

I am a new creature in you.

I will not play small any longer because I now serve you!

In Jesus name, I confess that I am saved.

AMEN

CONGRATULATIONS QUEEN! If you said that prayer for the first time or as a rededication of your faith; then we CELEBRATE with YOU! Welcome to the family of believers. Your Best Days are Ahead. It won't Always be easy, but it will most certainly be worth it! I AM a Living Witness.

I would love to pray for you if you just gave your life to Jesus Christ!

TEXT: SAVEDQUEEN to 31996 or email us at jesuscoffeeandprayer@gmail.com

We want to stand in the gap with you, pray for you, and encourage you in Christ!

* * * * * * * * * * * * * * * * * * *

If you would like Jesus, Coffee, and Prayer Christian Publishing House to Publish your next book or to become a Future Queen Coauthor TEXT: PublishME to 31996 for more details!!!

Be Sure to Follow us on FB & IG @JesusCoffeeandPrayer & Visit us @ www.jesuscoffeeandprayer.com

Queen, It's Time to Play Your Royal Position!

~Min. Nakita Davis

Thank you!

Special Thanks to Our Royal Court
Official Queen Sponsors

"May your hopes, dreams, standards, and business sales remain High like your heels!"
~Min. Nakita Davis

Queen
Keryn Dunmas
Real Estate Mogul

Queen Connect:
FB & IG @KerynDunmas
Virtual Reality Properties

Queen
Alishia Partee
Business Name: Partee Time Entertainment
Actress, Entrepreneur, Speaker, &
Future Bestselling Author

Queen Connect:
FB & IG @AlishiaPartee
https://parteetimeentertainment.com/

Queen
Wendy Thomas
Business Name: America's Best Kept Secret

Words to Live By:
"Once you know who you are, You don't have to worry anymore". - Nikki Giovanni

Queen Connect:
FB & IG @WendyRenee
www.wendyrenee.net

Queen
Donte Pickens
Business Name: Modest Glam Jewels Paparazzi Independent Consultant &
Future Bestselling Author

Favorite Scripture:
"For you shall go out with joy, And be led out with peace; The mountains and the hills Shall break forth into singing before you, And all the trees of the field shall clap their hands."
Isaiah 55:12 NKJV

Queen Connect:
FB & IG @ModestGlamJewels
www.ModestGlamJewels.com

Queen

Cassandra Hill

Business Name: Holistic Living Consulting LLC.

Favorite scripture

Beloved, I pray that you may prosper in all things, and be in health, just as your soul prospers. 3 John 1:2

Queen Connect:

www.facebook.com/livehealthyforlife

www.cassandraRhill.com

Queen
Natalie Bryan, LCSW
Best Selling Author of Body Talk &
Founder of P.E.A.R.L Inc.

Favorite Scripture:
"I can do all things through Christ who strengthens me." Philippians 4:13

Words to Live by:
"Every day that you wake up is another day to build, dream, and soar!"

Queen Connect
www.wearepearl.org
www.nakedandunafraid.net/natalie-bryan

Special Thanks

Jesus Christ~ My Lord & Savior~ You are my WHY!

Demecho Davis~ My hubby AKA My Papi

You are an amazing Husband and Dad! Our love~ team work~ & support for each other is one for the books!

Imani & Demecho Jr. AKA Jellybean

Mommy loves you always- You are brilliantly made in Jesus- Remember to Always SHINE Bright for His Glory!

Kim Honeycutt, Evangelist Latoya Mcdonald, Pastor Tammy Caesar~ Queens, I Thank God for your light, love, and support in this endeavor. You are truly your Sisters Keeper. May God Bless richly ALL that you touch!

Last but most certainly not least- my Queen Coauthors.

We set out to do something epic for the Kingdom of God and for the edification of our fellow Sisters in Christ. I am honored to say that we have done just that. I honor each of you for your honesty, transparency, and willingness to be vulnerable in the presence of strangers. Your words of wisdom, your journey, and faith will surely enrich the lives of Women worldwide.

This is only the beginning Queens and I SPEAK GREATER over your lives on this very day!

We started as authors but Now we are bonded by the love of Jesus Christ.

We are SISTERS!

Continue to Play Your Royal Position.

I Love You All

~Min. Nakita Davis

www.ingramcontent.com/pod-product-compliance
Lightning Source LLC
Chambersburg PA
CBHW031153160426
43193CB00008B/354